Our Little Secret, Revealed

Blythe Hardy

WESTBOW
PRESS®
A DIVISION OF THOMAS NELSON
& ZONDERVAN

Copyright © 2018 Blythe Hardy.

All rights reserved. No part of this book may be used or reproduced by any means, graphic, electronic, or mechanical, including photocopying, recording, taping or by any information storage retrieval system without the written permission of the author except in the case of brief quotations embodied in critical articles and reviews.

This book is a work of non-fiction. Unless otherwise noted, the author and the publisher make no explicit guarantees as to the accuracy of the information contained in this book and in some cases, names of people and places have been altered to protect their privacy.

WestBow Press books may be ordered through booksellers or by contacting:

WestBow Press
A Division of Thomas Nelson & Zondervan
1663 Liberty Drive
Bloomington, IN 47403
www.westbowpress.com
1 (866) 928-1240

Because of the dynamic nature of the Internet, any web addresses or links contained in this book may have changed since publication and may no longer be valid. The views expressed in this work are solely those of the author and do not necessarily reflect the views of the publisher, and the publisher hereby disclaims any responsibility for them.

Any people depicted in stock imagery provided by Getty Images are models, and such images are being used for illustrative purposes only. Certain stock imagery © Getty Images.

ISBN: 978-1-9736-3341-9 (sc)
ISBN: 978-1-9736-3342-6 (hc)
ISBN: 978-1-9736-3340-2 (e)

Library of Congress Control Number: 2018908024

Print information available on the last page.

WestBow Press rev. date: 09/14/2018

Contents

Acknowledgments vii
Preface ix

Chapter 1   The Early Years 1
Chapter 2   Good Little Boy 7
Chapter 3   Strike One 14
Chapter 4   Strike Two 19
Chapter 5   Home Run 46
Chapter 6   Brand New Ball Game 64
Chapter 7   It's Not My Fault, But … 76
Chapter 8   Post-Game Review 88
Chapter 9   Getting a Grip 99
Chapter 10 Restoring Relationships 106
Chapter 11 Facts and Myths 119

Bibliography and References 123
About the Author 125

Acknowledgments

Words are not sufficient for me to express my thanks to a few special people who were instrumental in this work:

1. First and foremost is my wife, Sabrina. You have been the epitome of the words *supportive* and *forgiving*. When I expected, through my clouded eyes, for you to completely abandon me for *Our Little Secret, Revealed*, you blew me away when you wrapped your arms around me. You have been used by God to completely free me from a chain that has figuratively been wrapped around my neck for over half a century. No matter what the future holds for us, you have given me a completely new perspective on what God meant when he had Paul pen the words in Romans 8:28, "… all things work together for good…" You will always be my motivation in that I want to love you like Christ also loved the church and *gave* Himself for it. God bless you, Sabrina!
2. Paul Roberts, After a battle with cancer, Paul has passed away since the initial submission of this work, his memory will go on. Paul was willing to listen to my blubbering and helped me struggle through a difficult healing process. I remember distinctly his words "You ought to write a book," followed by my comment, "You're crazy, I'm not a writer." Paul was a true and irreplaceable friend. I often

find myself reaching for the phone to get some of his wise counsel only to realize, he's in Heaven. If I had one friend like him, I'd be a rich man.

3. David Miller, thank you for being completely straightforward with me while going through our counseling. Your asking tough questions and being sensitive to both my needs and Sabrina's have been extremely helpful. God bless you.

4. Thelma Johnson, your keen eye and helpful suggestions have made the preliminary editing of this work a much easier process. Thank you for your willingness to hold in confidence the things written here until such time as it would be shared with all. God bless you.

5. Kelly Yarborough, thank you for your willingness to provide good, godly counsel. The assignment to write things down has ultimately led to the writing of this project. My prayer is that the things we victims of abuse have gone through will simply be another ingredient in the process of God working *all* things for good and that this work may lend itself to help others. God bless you!

6. Charlene R. Dalton, thank you for your direction in getting me the much-needed counseling. Maintaining a confidence that was kept between you, me, and your sister has been reassuring to me. God bless you!

7. Dr. John Landon, what can I say? You have been a mentor, advisor, and dear friend. You have shown me that one can indeed love unconditionally. When you tried to give me godly counsel, I didn't listen, but you continued to pray for me and saw me back to the fold after a miserable time in the proverbial pigpen. You will never know this side of heaven how much I've grown to appreciate and respect your instruction. If I had any idea you were as smart as you are, I would have spent a lot more time around you. God bless you.

Preface

Through a series of very undesirable events in my life, I have grown to truly believe and appreciate the scripture verse:
And we know that all things work together for good to them that love God, to them who are the called according to his purpose. (Romans 8:28)
I think we can all relate to the fact that we sometimes hear or read scriptures, and we *believe* it—but only on a superficial level. Then there are times when a particular verse, even one that we may have heard hundreds of times, jumps out and hits us like a brick; we can suddenly see how it applies to our lives.

I had struggled most of my life, wondering why some things were happening to me, just like the Apostle Paul in Romans chapter 7. I would wonder why I do the things I know I shouldn't and don't do the things I know I should. My intention in writing this book is to incorporate a very distasteful ingredient in my life to accomplish God's perfect will. I believe this publication could be extremely beneficial for helping others who have struggled with—or are currently dealing with—similar circumstances.

One particular counselor told me that I should begin writing things down as they were revealed to me. As I did that, I found that I couldn't stop writing. One thousand words turned into eighteen thousand in no time, and I continued on. The counselor also told me I should share my story in confidence with someone I could trust. When I shared my story with a dear friend, he suggested I write a book. "I'm no author," I exclaimed to him. Then I began thinking of the many people who have been adversely affected by similar experiences and who could possibly benefit from reading about what I've gone through. I have come to realize the truth in God's word when He had the apostle Paul pen these words:

And he said unto me, My grace is sufficient for thee: for my strength is made perfect in weakness. (2 Corinthians 12:9)

I realized that, while I have no claims to be an author, in *my* weakness God's strength can be made perfect. The culmination of this project should make it very clear to anyone who knows me that it was indeed *not* me but God who *perfected* this work.

I make no claims as a doctor, a PhD, a pastor, or even an author. I only know that I have been subjected to some horrific things that devastated my life. As a result of this ordeal, I have been counseled by pastors, authors, and professional counselors. My personal experience is that pastors are able to provide insight as it would apply *in theory*; however, the most effective words of wisdom given to me have been from those who have actually experienced similar circumstances.

Some of the events mentioned in this book are in direct conflict with Gods plan for anyone's life, in violation of God's laws in the area of purity, virtue, fidelity, and so forth. These things are not recorded for the purpose of dramatization, but rather to show how God has taken even the vilest things and has been working them in me for His good. I am not proud of any of the violations of God's law that are recorded in this book. The title chosen, *Our Little Secret, Revealed,* was selected because I was instructed by my abuser to keep a secret just between the two of us. This secret was revealed some fifty-five years later as a result of my wife's loving persistence.

As I considered the prospect of making these stories public, I had to seriously consider the effects they may have on me and my family. In going forward with the decision to share my story, I am risking complete alienation from some who may not understand the seriousness of the impact on men who have been sexually abused as children. In no way do I intend to come across in a braggadocious manner, but I merely attempt to convey the detrimental effects an experience like this can have.

My prayer is that, if you are experiencing some of the things portrayed in this book, you will read all the way to the end. The first half deals with things that happened to me and my inappropriate behavior, but the last half explains how you can become free from *any* addiction you may be struggling with.

Scriptures quoted in this book are taken from the Authorized King James Version of the Holy Bible.

Chapter 1

The Early Years

Off to the West Coast

I was born in a small rural town in the state of Colorado. When most people think of Colorado, their minds go to the beautiful Rocky Mountains, the Royal Gorge, Pikes Peak, and so forth. This does not describe my hometown at all. I like to say that my hometown is more like a part of Kansas that just likes to call itself Colorado. The closest "mountains" are a place called The Bluffs just to the southeast of town. They look like a couple of anthills off in the distance.

When I was still very young (fourteen months old), my father was offered and accepted a job in Southern California working as a Customer Engineer for a computer company. We left our hometown, got on a train, and relocated to Southern California. Our first residence was an apartment in a place called The Palms. It was a small, single-level apartment complex with maybe twenty-four units, but some cousins and good friends lived there too. It was also nice in that we had our own backyard and lots of places to play. Just on the other side of the brick wall in our backyard was the Los Angeles river. It very rarely had any water, but it was fun to play on the riverbank. We would catch horned toads and other critters that were intriguing to little boys.

Another perk was that we lived only a few short miles from a place called Chavez Ravine. This is where the Brooklyn Dodgers eventually relocated after moving from New York in 1958. Dodger Stadium was constructed at this site and opened in 1962. Although we moved from The Palms the first year Dodger Stadium opened, I can still recall hearing the roar of the crowd from our home during those first months the Dodgers were there. Because of this early exposure, I became an avid Dodger fan at a very young age and have been one ever since. I can remember going to bed at night with a transistor radio earpiece in my ear, listening to the melodious voice of the Dodgers' hall of fame broadcaster, Vin Scully.

When I was five years old I began kindergarten not too far from our home. This was a much different time in that we could walk about six blocks to school in the city of Los Angeles. You wouldn't think of doing that in today's world. One year, when my older brother was six and I was only four years old, we walked six or seven blocks to one of the major boulevards in town to buy a gift for my mom's birthday.

We lived in The Palms for four or five years, through my completion of first grade. We then relocated to a suburban town in the San Gabriel Valley about twenty-six miles east of Los Angeles. This was not a very prestigious area, but my father had taken an opportunity to buy a fixer upper for between ten and twelve thousand dollars—*yes*, only ten to twelve thousand dollars. I remember in the backyard there were weeds literally from one fence to the other. It was not at all uncommon on a Saturday afternoon for my two brothers, my dad, and me to spend hours pulling weeds. We would probably be listening to the Dodger game on the radio as they battled Willie Mays, Willie McCovey, the Alou Brothers, Jimmy Davenport, Juan Marichal, and the rest of our rivals from the north, the Giants of San Francisco.

The picture portrayed here is hopefully one of a normal lifestyle for a little boy in a very functional home. My father worked the midnight shift, which allowed him to be there nearly all the time that I was at home. When I woke up in the morning, Dad was getting home from work. When I went to school, Dad went to sleep. When I got home from school, Dad was waking from his sleep, and when I went to bed, Dad would get his power nap prior to going back to work for the night. Up until I was about ten or eleven, I didn't even realize he had a job because he was always home.

Sports were promoted around our house. We all played Little League baseball, Pop Warner football, and so on. Dad was a pitcher on a fast-pitch softball team so many times I would put on the glove and play catch with him in the backyard. It was a picture perfect *Ozzie and Harriet*, *Father Knows Best*, or *Leave It to Beaver* kind of life.

Weekends at Grandma's House

My mom's dad died when she was just a teenager, and my grandma remarried the man I knew as Granddad. During my early childhood, Grandma and Granddad lived only a few miles away, so we would go to their house nearly every weekend to visit. Several cousins also lived in the area, so it was not at all unusual to have a mini-reunion with two or three dozen people on any given weekend at Grandma's house.

I also had two uncles and two aunts who were still living at Grandma's house. One of my uncles was only a couple of years older than me, and I looked up to him as I would an older brother. I tried to do some of the same things he did, such as card tricks (he taught me how to shuffle a deck of cards), strumming the guitar, trying to play a harmonica, riding motorcycles, and playing pranks. I trusted him much like I would trust my older brother.

Hiding Places

There was generally quite a bit of commotion around the house with some cousins playing typical childhood games like stickball and hide and seek. The yard had several trees and shrubs that presented opportune places to hide. We sometimes played war games and these places were good for make shift forts. There were also other hiding places in the yard where one could get lost if he or she really wanted to.

I was around nine or ten years of age when I had the first memory of my uncle coercing me into doing things that I knew deep down were wrong, but again, I looked up to him. He took me to one of those hiding places and began touching, fondling, and doing other things to me that I knew were inappropriate. Even though I knew it was wrong, it was an extremely pleasurable sensation from a physical standpoint, and, as a normal young boy, I enjoyed it.

In His Defense

As I was writing this I was contemplating the idea that an 8 year old (my uncle) could be committing abuse of this nature. I began to wonder if it was possible that he too was being abused. Since the initiation of this book I have discovered that there was another uncle (by marriage) who had committed pedafile acts on his step-children (my cousins). I began to consider that, while I do remember that uncle, I have no recollection of him ever touching me. It is very possible that he introduced this behavior to my abuser. Later on in this story there is mention of a shadow in my mind that I remember seeing but have been unable to identify. While I have no conclusive evidence, this uncle may very well be that shadow.

Because of this pleasurable feeling, I concluded that, at least to some extent, this must be partially my fault. Although the physical feelings were enjoyable, I also knew that it was wrong, which caused much confusion in my preadolescent mind. It was at this time that I was introduced to a sexual environment that was totally contrary to God's plan of sexual enjoyment between married couples.

While this is my first recollection of this type of experience, as I look back, I can more accurately place the first incident a few years earlier. I remember being in my bedroom when we lived at The Palms, and although I don't remember doing anything there, I do remember my uncle making the comment, "We are going to go to hell for the things we are doing." This comment and where it took place lead me to consider that this abuse had begun when I was six or seven years of age. Remember, we lived in The Palms until I was around seven years old, and that is where my uncle made the comment.

This weekend-at-grandma's routine went on until they moved to a different state some six or seven years after the initial abuse. As I was doing research regarding the effects on adult men who had been sexually abused as children, I discovered that one of the factors that determines the extent of the adverse effects is the age at which the abuse began and how long it continued.

My regular weekend routine was to go to grandma's house, where my uncle would entice me to one of those hiding places, where we would explore that desirable physical sensation. Although the experience was physically enjoyable, my uncle's insistence that it would be "our little secret" was a tip-off to me that it was not appropriate behavior. Because I knew deep down that it was wrong, and because I did not want to get into trouble, I was afraid to tell anyone, especially my parents. So I kept what became "our little secret" between my uncle and me hidden in my heart.

Continuing the "Lifestyle"

Grandma and Granddad moved to another state when I was young, and my uncle went with them. I was probably between ten and twelve years old when they moved. As a result of the introduction to this lifestyle at a very early age, and the enjoyable physical sensation I had experienced, I sought out other adolescents who had been launched into a similar lifestyle. I subsequently continued to satisfy my lustful desires.

I believe that God gives us all an innate sense of right and wrong. My abuser was a close relative, my uncle, who was not that much older than me, but I still looked up to him. As a little boy, I was extremely vulnerable and felt virtually powerless to challenge his advances. Nevertheless, as I grew into a man, I understood that this was wrong and was able to make the necessary change. I had a choice either to continue doing what I knew was wrong or to turn from this ungodly lifestyle. Unfortunately, I fell for the line of the sixties: "If it feels good, do it." I subsequently held on to this secret for over a half a century.

Chapter 2

Good Little Boy

Fire Insurance

During our first summer in the suburbs, a dear lady came by our house and asked us boys if we'd like to attend DVBS at a little church on the corner. I didn't even know what DVBS meant (daily vacation Bible school), but the lady said they would have cookies, punch, and games. That sounded like fun, so we went.

After a week of DVBS, I continued attending this little church on the corner and have been attending a church of like faith regularly (off and on) ever since, all the while keeping "our little secret." I learned from experience that just because one regularly attends a good church does not mean one is a Christian.

We meet many people going through this thing called life, and some have more impact on us than others, both negative and positive. Mrs. Bonnie Sanger is the lady who came by and invited us three little boys to DVBS, and she has been a best friend of our whole family ever since. On occasion, I have sought counsel from Mrs. Sanger, only to usually pay no heed to her wise advice.

I went to church one summer on a Sunday evening when I was twelve years old, and I heard my pastor preach a sermon about hell. If I heard nothing else, I definitely knew that hell was a place

I did *not* want to go. On our way home from church that night, I could see a fire in the nearby mountains, and it looked as though the flames were coming right down the road to my house. I was very restless and could not sleep, so I shared this concern with my mother. She called our pastor, and he came over to our house late that night. He showed me, from the Bible, how I could know that, when I die, heaven could be my home. He explained these four easy steps referred to as "The Roman's Road" to heaven:

1. Realize you are a sinner. For all have sinned, and come short of the glory of God; (Romans 3:23).
2. Realize that there is a penalty for our sin. For the wages of sin is death; (Romans 6:23a).
3. Realize that God made that payment through His son, Jesus Christ. But God commendeth His love toward us, in that, while we were yet sinners, Christ died for us. (Romans 5:8).
4. Receive this free gift of salvation. That if thou shalt confess with thy mouth the Lord Jesus, and shalt believe in thine heart that God hath raised Him from the dead, thou shalt be saved. For with the heart man believeth unto righteousness; and with the mouth confession is made unto salvation. For whosoever shall call upon the name of the Lord shall be saved. (Romans 10:9–10, 13)

To a twelve-year-old, this sounded like a good, simple formula to go to heaven, so I prayed what some refer to as: "The Sinner's Prayer". After following these steps, however, my lifestyle didn't change when it came to the physical, sexual experiences I had been enjoying. That's okay, though, because I now had my fire insurance, so I was covered.

Disaster Is Imminent

Even as I am writing this, I can't help but wonder what kind of sexual lifestyle a twelve-year-old could possibly have. I had been introduced to a sexual environment that was intended to be reserved for married couples. I thought of an analogy that I believe is extremely applicable:

Introducing a six-year-old to a sexual environment that is reserved for married couples is like giving a six-year-old the keys to your car. In each case, disaster is imminent.

As a six-year-old, I had been given the keys to the car and was sitting in the driver's seat, in a manner of speaking, headed to a disastrous end result.

As I grew into my preteen and teen years, even after my uncle moved away, I found there were other adolescent boys who enjoyed this same kind of exploration. Adolescent bodies are changing in a way that causes much curiosity. As normal young boys, we were simply curious about all these changes taking place. But one thing led to another, and just like with my uncle, we would find hiding places where we could go, stimulate, and satisfy each other physically. All this took place while I was attending church every Sunday, continually playing the role of a good little boy.

As I look back, I am sincerely grieved at the fact that I had misrepresented our Lord and Savior. I proclaimed that I was a Christian, all the while continuing in the sin that was introduced to me by my uncle as a little boy. A particular scripture verse comes to mind, one I have even taught in the junior high Sunday school class:

> But I keep under my body, and bring it into subjection: lest that by any means, when I have preached to others, I myself should be a castaway. (1 Corinthians 9:27)

The word *castaway* in this context refers to being disqualified. I had been playing the role of a good little boy, going to Sunday school and church, but my lifestyle had deemed me disqualified to preach to others. How could I possibly witness to my peers when I was doing things that were obviously against God's will? Probably a more familiar term, and one that I had epitomized, is a *hypocrite*.

Girls, Girls, Girls

One of the effects of sexual addiction is much like that of any other addiction: the need to reach for a higher high, to explore new levels of the addiction. For example, a drug addict might start with an occasional high from marijuana, then move on to pills, and then the next thing you know, he or she is hooked on heroin or crack cocaine. An alcoholic might move from an occasional beer to a case a day and then on to hard liquor.

Unfortunately, society sometimes doesn't recognize sex as a legitimate addiction. Some say, "He's just a playboy, Don Juan, or Casanova." There seems to be a reluctance to accept the fact that this is also a serious addiction. Just as the alcoholic and drug addict are constantly seeking a new high, the sex addict also cannot seem to find satisfaction and continually seeks something new.

When I got into my teen years, my natural affections turned to girls, or more accurately, what I could get from girls. Through my high school years, I dated several girls but was more interested in fulfilling that lustful desire than in having a normal, healthy, God-pleasing relationship. It wasn't until I was a senior in high school that I had my first intimate encounter with Susan Boyles. Some would refer to this as "losing my virginity."

This too was a new sensation, or high, from a physical standpoint, and because of my warped sense of what was normal, it merely fed into my lustful desires more and more. Coincidently, or perhaps conveniently, Susan attended our church primarily to escape her older brother's sexually abusive advances.

I remember sneaking in through her bedroom window in the middle of the night to visit. Her brother was an entertainer at a nightclub and didn't come home until the very early hours of the morning. I was working the midnight shift for a fast food restaurant and would go to her house during my lunch break just to spend a few lascivious moments, and then go back to work. Studies have shown that adult men who were abused as children often take unnecessary risks. This is now even more evident to me as I look back on this particular time of my life.

After high school, I attended Bible college, mainly to find girls. My lifestyle was generally the same except, because of my newfound "normal" attraction to girls, my need for participation with men had diminished. One of the girls once referred to me as a player, and I guess that's what you could call it. I went out with many different girls and had only one real intention in mind. I dated girls from my church and from Bible college with no regard to the harmful effects I was destined to cause. This became a very common tendency as I look back; I had become extremely narcissistic, not considering at all what damage I may cause others, having complete disregard for the feelings and long-term effects I was having on them.

Susan and I continued to date when we could, and after a period of time, we eventually became engaged. This turned out to be anything but the perfect arrangement, as her brother was adamantly opposed to Susan interacting with anyone. After trying to make a go of it, sneaking around behind his back for several months, she decided to break it off "for my sake." Susan had related to me that her brother had been abusing her for many years and that he would not allow her to see anyone.

Not long after the breakup, she moved away and I didn't hear from her for a long time. She did eventually leave California and married someone who took her away from her abusive brother.

Later, I met a girl who was visiting for the summer from another state. Some of her family had recently moved to California, and this was an opportunity for her to see some of the exciting things California has to offer. While she was there for summer break, we dated and became very close. As summer came to an end, she moved back home to the Midwest, but we continued to communicate through phone calls and letters. I remember plugging $2.50 to $3.00 worth of quarters into a pay phone to call her long distance. I really thought I had found the one and had possibly kicked this thing.

A couple years later, she and her parents moved to the central coast of California, and we were able to see each other pretty frequently. I had moved on to dating other girls while she was gone, so it was a little awkward for me at first. Eventually I did filter out the others and eventually asked her father for her hand in marriage. After extensive scrutiny, he gave me permission, and I asked her to marry me. She said yes, and we were engaged.

Her parents were very godly people who definitely had her best interests in mind. I was visiting on one particular occasion, and her parents walked in while we were engaged in some inappropriate fondling. They eventually determined that it was not a good match, so the engagement was broken off.

I had dated Carolyn Rodriquez intermittently, but it was not really exclusive. It seems that she was what one might call a *fallback girl*. If I had no date for a Friday or Saturday night, I could call her. I continued being the player; after all, there are a lot of fish in the sea, right? And I did so love to fish. Eventually, some of the girls began to move away, get married, or whatever, so my pool was depleting—and I wasn't getting any younger.

I continued to date some girls just for the sake of having something to do on a Friday or Saturday night, and then one day, a friend asked me, "Why don't you quit messing around and just marry Carolyn Rodriquez?" At first, I thought, *You've got to be out of your mind*, but as she and I began to date more and more, and as the other prospects continued to dwindle away, I hoped that I could finally beat this thing and eventually have guilt-free sex, so

I asked Carolyn to marry me. She said yes and we began making plans for the wedding.

All this time when I was being the player, I continued to attend church regularly. I even taught some Sunday school classes and sang in the choir, continuing to hang on to my status of that good little boy.

Chapter 3

Strike One

Not long after Carolyn and I were married, I realized she was nowhere near as interested in the intimate physical pleasures designed for married couples as I was. Carolyn was a very beautiful woman but our personalities were almost completely opposite as she displayed very dominant traits while I was always happy-go-lucky and extremely passive.

One area particularly comes to mind: I never really wanted to be the money manager of the home, so Carolyn took on that responsibility. I remember, being the passive husband I was, asking her, "Can I *please* have five dollars so I can go play golf?" There is a term to describe my lack of backbone; some people refer to it as being *henpecked,* and man was I ever!

This passivity gave me feelings of inadequacy and low self-esteem along with several other negative effects that stemmed from the childhood sexual abuse. I also allowed myself to be very easily manipulated into doing things I really didn't want to do, much like how my uncle manipulated me into the initial sexual abuse. All of these factors combined led to continual outbursts of anger aimed mostly at my wife. As I look back, once again I can see how much disregard I had for her feelings, along with the well-being of my children.

Carolyn and I met when she began coming to our church youth group. She came with a couple of her friends who were escaping different domestic issues by coming to church. Through the years, I have found this to be a very common occurrence throughout church youth groups. My prayer is that this book will also help in these cases. The consequences of the sexual abuse I had experienced as a child contributed to frustration. This led to repeated outbursts of anger aimed mainly at Carolyn, which, in turn affected the kids drastically.

Taking all these things into consideration, I still had this insatiable need to provide for my addiction so I pursued a lady at work. She was divorced, and we were physically attracted to each other. She knew I was married, but I convinced her that I was just "not getting it" at home, and she seemed to be okay with that. We met a few times; some of the encounters were actually at work, in the stairwells or in a secret room. This all now seems particularly familiar, as my uncle was also constantly looking for those secret hiding places.

NOTE: I am in no way trying to excuse my actions because of anything that happened to me. I have since come to recognize the fact that, as an adult, I need to take responsibility for my own actions.

Sometimes, woman's companionship was not readily available. With my insatiable sexual appetite driving me, I recalled my preadolescent experiences; I knew there were men at work who were fond of men, so I secretly approached some who I thought might be willing to have a casual encounter to provide immediate gratification for me. Thinking back, I never did have any homosexual feelings. If given an option, I would always choose a woman's companionship over a man's. Again, that is nothing to boast about, but just an observation.

Rationalize, Rationalize

I worked for a major company in Southern California and was scheduled to make a business trip to the northern part of the state. I went to attend a three-week class, returning home each weekend during the class. When I arrived at the airport and got checked into my hotel, I felt like a bird that had been let out of its cage. After all, I would not be under the dominant reign of my wife and could do whatever I pleased—no need to ask for that five dollars. Fortunately, I had to provide receipts only to the company, and not to Carolyn.

During the first week of my training, I went to dinner with one of my brothers, who just happened to be there on business also. We were sitting at our table talking about the kids, mom and dad, work, and so on, when a woman entered the restaurant. She caught my attention immediately, and I kept glancing over at her table like a puppy-love-stricken teenager hoping she might notice me too.

After dinner, I opened my organizer and pretended to be documenting my expenses. I couldn't let my brother think I was trying to pick up this woman; after all, I was married. Instead of recording my expenses I was actually jotting down a message on a yellow sticky note. The message read something like this: "Would like to meet you, please call me at [hotel phone number]." After leaving the table, I "accidentally" and conveniently bumped into her chair and stuck the note on it. I left the restaurant thinking to myself, *There is no way in the world she is even going to find that note, let alone call me!*

Well, about 11:00 that night, the phone rang; it was Erma Mendoza. She told me that the waitress had seen the note and given it to her. The first thing she asked me was "Are you married?" *Uh-oh*, I thought, and then I began to quickly rationalize that, after these three weeks, I'd never see her again, so... "No, I'm not married."

I had taken a detrimental leap down a slippery slope that would lead me to do some unconscionable things. The opportunity arose, and that opened the door for me; I took advantage of the opportunity, and I had an affair.

When I had first gotten married, I'd had several preconceived notions regarding what to expect in bed. Of course, with my premature introduction to a sexual environment, I didn't know what normal really looked like. At first I thought maybe it was just that Carolyn and I were young and inexperienced. Maybe I was just some kind of sex-crazed maniac with unreal expectations, or maybe I was just oversexed.

Erma and I met several times over the three weeks of this business trip, both at her apartment and in my hotel room. I don't know if it was just the excitement of the sin—after all, sin is pleasurable for a season according to Hebrews 11:24-26 However, I couldn't help but think to myself, *This is the kind of sensation I was anticipating on my wedding night.*

One thing I've noticed is that because of my early exposure and subsequent sexual addiction, I had developed my own perception of what was normal, sexually speaking, and it was completely out of focus. The addiction had caused me to constantly seek that "new high," to try something different. This would eventually make it difficult for me to diagnose exactly what a normal love life should look like.

After the three weeks were over on the day I was to fly home, Erma asked me again, "Are you married?" I rationalized once more—*I'll never see this woman again*—so I told her I was. She then confessed to me that she knew deep down all along that I was. I guess for some reason that made me feel a little less guilty about the whole thing.

Total Disregard

A couple weeks after my business trip, I went right back to

having feelings of frustration. Eventually, I stood up to my wife and told her that I'd had an affair while in Northern California. Naturally, she exploded. "*I hate you!*" she exclaimed. After several weeks of arguing, answering questions, and making excuses and accusations, Carolyn and I finally decided that we should seek a marriage counselor, and we did.

Initially, we sought counsel from one of the staff members at our church. He was the teacher who taught our class for young married couples. He helped to some extent, but eventually he recommended that we look for someone more experienced with couples counseling, and we did.

By the time we made the decision to get help, too many other things had happened—a lot of finger pointing and so much hurt that some would say "too much water under the bridge." It was clear after only two or three sessions that we were not in marriage counseling at all, but rather divorce counseling. We filed and divorced after eleven years of marriage and two children.

Let me be very clear in sharing that none of the events described above are in any way the fault of my wife or of anyone else other than myself. While it is true that I was a victim of sexual abuse as a child, as an adult, I have had the ability to turn from my lifestyle and let God direct my paths. Even so, I continually ignored the obvious bells and whistles that were going off in my life; I just continued to ignore the obvious signs.

Looking back, I can see my habitual, total disregard for the feelings of and long-term effects on the people in my life: Erma Mendoza, my wife, my children, even my brother. I've also observed that, just like the preachers continually preach, after the first time, it gets easier and easier to continue in whatever sin you are involved. Your heart tends to become callous to the moving of the Holy Spirit. Don't wait to find yourself in the proverbial pigpen to turn around. You can kick this thing (whatever that might be in your life).

Chapter 4

Strike Two

A Predator

Not long after the dissolution of my first marriage, I began to pursue others who would help feed my addiction. Even as I'm writing this, I have the feeling of a predator simply looking to satisfy my selfish, fleshly desires with no consideration for others. I met a few women, but as a result of my impatient urge to be satisfied and not wanting to wait for the right woman, I went back to the preadolescent activity of hooking up with men to fulfill my lustful needs.

When I look back on the experience, I have come to the conclusion that the partner with whom I was engaging in this wickedness—whether woman or man—had nothing to do with the person. To me, he or she served simply as a tool to bring about a selfish gratification. As with any addiction, the need to reach for a new high was also present in my situation. It seemed that this interaction with both men and women just did not satisfy my increasing obsession for inappropriate physical pleasure.

After a reasonably short time, I did meet another woman to whom I was attracted. Geneva Munoz was fun to be around, but she was also completely uninhibited regarding physically intimate matters. Geneva and I had many things in common. She also had two young children similar in age to my own children, and we just seemed to hit it off. When I say we "hit it off," I refer to that as it would pertain to friendship, but even more so in the area of physical attraction.

Modus Operandi—Mode of Operation

After living together for a period of time, eventually I decided that I should move on, so I looked for an affordable place to stay. I found a bachelor pad in a small town near the foothills and moved there. This move had nothing to do with any sudden development of scruples, nor was there any real moral significance. Relocation was actually rather convenient for me as the initial passion with Geneva had cooled down a little, and I could be a player once again. I continued to meet other women and occasionally sought out men as well. This wicked lifestyle developed into my routine.

My *modus operandi* progressed—or rather regressed—into looking for a willing woman; then, if that took too long, I would hunt down a man who wanted to provide the desired instant gratification. After all, there was no commitment in doing that. Another one of the ramifications of men being sexually abused as children is the inability to make and keep commitments.

After some time, and to some extent after I tired of playing this game, I decided to get serious again with Geneva. After a period of time with her exclusively, I asked her children if it would be okay for me to ask their mother to marry me. After obtaining their consent, I asked Geneva and she said yes, so we were married.

After a couple years of marriage, we purchased a house in the suburbs, and everything seemed to be going well. *Maybe I've found* the one *and have finally kicked this thing,* I thought. Geneva was much more interested and willing to participate in the pleasurable parts of marriage, so maybe I finally had my cake and could eat it too, so to speak. We also found a church in the area and became regular members; we even played on the softball team and made a lot of new church friends.

But as with any addiction, I just couldn't get enough, so I began to wander again, all the while keeping "our little secret." Again, I did not limit my search to women but also sought out men who were willing (and actually wanted) to give gratification, sticking to my mode of operation.

Back to Northern California

About a year after we bought our house, I was presented with an opportunity for a promotion and transfer to Northern California. At that time, many associates were being redeployed or laid off at work, so Geneva and I agreed that I should accept the offer. Geneva had a good job as a teacher, and she couldn't just pick up and leave in the middle of a school year. So I went on ahead and looked for housing in a good area, schools for the kids, and potential job opportunities for my wife—and, of course, a good church to attend.

On the day I left, while I was saying my goodbyes in the driveway, Geneva saw some paraphernalia that had fallen out of my pocket. It was condoms. She asked what that was all about, and I told her I'd found them on the sidewalk and was going to throw them away or some other lame explanation—I really don't even remember. My inability to be honest was a problem I have had since this all began.

I got in the car drove some four hundred miles up the coast to the San Francisco Bay Area. I had arranged to rent a room from an associate who worked in the same area, so I settled in his home in the East Bay.

This associate was co-owner of this house, and the other owner had a girlfriend who was also staying there. She was only about twenty years old and pretty ditzy. I recall one day when I came home from work, she gave me a message that my daughter had called, and I asked, "Which one? I've got four."

She said, "Duh, I don't know." This led to a rather heated discussion on how to take a message for someone.

After only about a month, things weren't working out with this other roommate, so I moved into a motel not far away, still in the East Bay. The company was paying for my relocation expenses, so the motel arrangement would work for me temporarily. While staying there, I continued to look for an apartment, a job for my wife, and a good church.

Not long after I moved into the motel, I began to think about Erma Mendoza, the lady I had met on my business trip several years before. I looked her up and was able to contact her, and we arranged to meet. The first thing she asked me was, "Are you still married?" Well, I considered that, since I was not married to the same woman, I could answer no. So we picked up right where we had left off.

I was a little concerned about this because I knew I was not going to be around for just three weeks like before. But the family wasn't scheduled to move up for another four months or so. So I thought, *Sure, I can do this*. You have probably noticed the definite trend of dishonesty, another detrimental ramification of being abused as a child.

Small Groups

After the family moved and we got settled in, I did come clean with Erma Mendoza and I began my life with Geneva and her two children. When we were all together again, things seemed to be going pretty well. I had found a good church and we began attending. The church had a program where groups of people met in homes on different nights throughout the week. They were referred to as "Small Groups". We hosted one of the "Small Groups" in our apartment one night each week.

OUR LITTLE SECRET, REVEALED

After a period of time, I once again began seeking instant gratification elsewhere. There were some women at work who showed an interest, and in my frame of mind, I didn't need to be shown a lot of interest to seek out a secret place. With women and men alike, my appetite to continually reach for a bigger high had gotten completely out of control. Again, as with any addiction, the vice has you under its spell, seizing your ability to think and act rationally. (And again, I'm not making excuses.)

For some reason—maybe how simple it was to find someone, I'm not sure—I got to the point where it actually alarmed me to even think about my fall into this wicked lifestyle. I had, up to that point, never even associated my inability to kick this thing with the abuse of my childhood. I simply thought that I must be overzealous about these physical pleasures, or that there must be some other root cause. "Our little secret" had never been brought up, even in my own mind, as a possible cause of this perverse lifestyle.

Occasionally, men would actually approach me and, depending on whether or not a woman was readily available, I would either decline or accept their advances. I got to the point that I thought, in my warped sense of right and wrong, that I was providing a service as well as receiving this instant gratification.

All of this immoral and ungodly behavior was happening while I was ironically attending a church there in the neighborhood. We were actually hosting "small groups" in our first-floor apartment while I was participating in this despicable lifestyle, literally in the apartment right above our meeting place.

Once again, I showed that I had no regard for the feelings of and long-term effects on my wife, or for those participating with me, or—most disconcerting to me now—for the ones that I should have been showing the love and grace of Jesus *through* my life. Once again, this scripture rings out:

But I keep under my body, and bring it into subjection: lest that by any means, when I have preached to others, I myself should be a castaway. (1 Corinthians 9:27)

I had definitely disqualified myself through my dishonorable testimony and my despicable and hypocritical lifestyle.

New Career, Diminishing Lifestyle

After about seven years working in the new department, and after spending twenty-six years with this major company, my job was being eliminated. I accepted a severance package and began looking for another job. I had already been casually looking, as it was obvious that my job was a short-term assignment. I found an opportunity as a general manager in the hospitality industry. I genuinely did enjoy working with people and considered myself a hospitable person, but this position lent itself to all kinds of opportunities for my perverse way of life.

I have an example of the unrelenting need to reach for a new high. As a relief general manager, I was assigned to travel from one hotel to another while the resident managers went on vacations. While I was at one property for a couple of weeks, I started searching the internet. The constant need to reach for something new had caught up with me again. It was as though a new lure was dangled in front of me, and like a hungry bass, I gobbled up the bait.

I saw an ad from a man and wife who were looking for someone to "join in" with them. I responded, we met, and they came to the hotel, where we all engaged in what had become a new high for me, and a new low in my fall down this ungodly path.

NOTE: As I stated in the Preface to this book, I am merely attempting to depict how once you fall into this addiction, there seems to be no limit to where you might go. I am not proud of any of these things.

Perhaps, while you are reading this, a light bulb has come on in your mind. These examples may have helped you understand why you are involved in some of the things you may be doing. If so, please continue reading; there is a light at the end of the tunnel, and you can kick your habit too.

I worked for a couple different hotel management companies before eventually being offered a position as the general manager of a motel only about five minutes from the ocean. What an opportunity! This was a quaint little beach town on the central coast where the climate offers an average high of 85 degrees in the summer and 67 in the winter. I remember thinking to myself, and I even made this statement to my parents, "This has got to be as good as it gets." I really thought at this point that I had finally conquered this thing.

However ...

After eleven years of marriage to Geneva Munoz, I was searching the internet one day and found Classmates, a website for reconnecting with old friends, coworkers, classmates and so on. I did some searching and found several friends, and then I began thinking about Susan Boyles and wondered how she was doing. Remember: Susan was the girl I had been engaged to, but her brother had forbidden us from seeing each other. I hadn't heard anything from her since she had gotten away from her brother and married.

After searching this website, I found her and sent a message just to see how she was doing. As it turned out, her husband had passed away a few years earlier. I saw this as an opportunity to rekindle an old flame.

Can you see what was happening here? I was going to rekindle an old flame while I was still married! The depths to which I fell are shocking even to me as I tell of it now.

After a lengthy period of time corresponding back and forth, we decided to meet. The tricky thing about this meeting was that I lived in California and Susan lived halfway across the country, some 2,100 miles away.

Gone Fishing?

I thought a fishing trip to the Gulf of Mexico would be the perfect scheme. I told my wife that a friend of mine in Northern California was planning such a trip and wanted to know if I could go with him. I had to call my friend to see if he would back me up on my story. Notice again the persistent deceit, another shortcoming that is common among men who were sexually abused as children.

This could work; after all, Geneva knew how much I loved to fish. As I began to make my deceitful plans, Geneva realized there was something fishy about this fishing trip, so she called to consult a dear friend, Dr. John Landon.

Not long after her consultation, Dr. Landon called and asked me what I was up to. He tried to caution me about what Geneva knew I was going to do. After listening to him for a few minutes, I told him (in a nutshell) to mind his own business and that "I know what I'm doing," and then I proceeded to go on my fishing trip.

NOTE: Dr. Landon had been a much admired and respected voice of counsel to me since I was about fourteen years old. The effects of what had happened led to my total disregard for the feelings of and long-term effects on others, including Dr. Landon. With this conversation, I had taken it a step further, completely abandoning my long-term friendship with him.

After my stint in the proverbial pig pen, I continually thought about how I had disregarded the feelings and long-term effects that I had caused in others: my wife, her kids, my parents, my friend from Northern California, and my dear friend Dr. Landon.

I have since followed advice from this respected mentor, which has, in due course, led to this very publication. I'd like to just take a brief minute out of this story to say this: Thank you, Dr. John, for your continued prayers and for not giving up on me. You are and will always be a much-loved friend and voice of counsel. May God bless you!

From a Fishing Trip to the Proverbial Pigpen

I met Susan Boyles at a small town on the Gulf of Mexico, and we went straight to a room she had secured just for the occasion. I spent a week with her there, then returned home to basically tell my wife that I was leaving her and moving halfway across the country, once again having no regard for the feelings of or long-term effects on others. I devastated Geneva, her kids, her family, my family, my dear friend, and on and on it goes.

While living in the proverbial pigpen from Luke 15:11–32, several things happened that resulted in a few return trips to California. Not long after I made the move, my father, living in Southern California, suffered a heart attack, but he was doing okay according to my mother.

About three days after his heart attack, dad's belly began to swell from an abscess in his colon. The doctors informed us that dad might very well not make it through major surgery right on the heels of a heart attack. I flew back to be with him and Mom.

When I arrived at the hospital, dad seemed to be doing pretty well. He was in good humor, and I recall him asking me if I wanted to see his scar. Due to my previous history of fainting at the mere sight of blood, I suggested that I probably should pass on that.

I flew back to the proverbial pigpen and went back to my job at the hotel. I started feeling like I was simply being manipulated to be a fix-it man around Susan's house. As I look back, being manipulated is one of the things I've been plagued with, going back to my uncle's initial manipulation.

Her house had a pretty large backyard that I was of course expected to take care of. There was also a pretty large game room—around 400 square feet—with a television, games, pool table, and other types of entertainment. I was given the task of laying laminate wood flooring. Another of the jobs assigned to me was installing double, French-style doors.

It was becoming obvious to me that I had made a big mistake leaving California. Nevertheless, I kept trying to make the best of the situation, knowing full well that it was not the will of God.

Several months after my father's colon surgery, my dad's brother passed away. Two days later, his sister died, at which point I decided to make my second trip back home to be with my father. By this time, dad had seen the death of two siblings in a matter of just a few days. He also had experienced two heart attacks himself and had had an abscess requiring surgery to remove more than a foot of his colon.

I flew into Los Angeles International Airport and made the drive to the San Gabriel Valley. I was able to spend time with my father and attend my aunt's funeral. My father knew I was not following the will of God. He reassured me that he loved me no matter what was going on, and that he always would.

My brothers were both reminiscing about getting spankings for different things. They were laughing about some of the crazy things they had done to bring on such discipline. I was listening and could not remember getting too many spankings myself so I asked, "where was I when all these spankings were going on"? Dad responded, "you were sneaky". He was right and my life was a shambles because of that ability to evade trouble and keep secrets.

I had one of my favorite memories with dad during that visit, but that is going to have to be in another book.

About five or six days after my return to the proverbial pigpen,

I received a call from my older brother telling me that the doctors were giving Dad only about three days to live.

I explained to Susan that I needed to fly back to be with my mom and see my father before his passing. "You were going to clean up the backyard for the graduation party, who's going to do that?" she asked. I told her that I was terribly sorry my dad's dying was interfering with graduation plans, but I was going to California. Her response was quite appalling as I think about it, but helped me understand some things that happened upon my return from California.

I flew into the airport in the morning. Dad was unconscious when I got to the house, and he never did show any signs of awareness. I remember talking to my father while holding his hands. Dad and mom were ministers to the deaf for approximately 31 years and dad had shown many deaf people how to be saved with the use of those hands. My father passed away around ten o'clock that night. He was never told about *Our Little Secret, Revealed*, but in his last days, he knew that I was not in the perfect will of God, and his desire was for me to make it right.

During the night, I penned a poem about Dad and his influence on so many deaf people throughout his life. On the day of his funeral, I read this poem. There were numerous deaf in attendance as I continued to play the role of the good little boy:

The Hands of a Man

>What can you tell by the hands of a man,
>can you see if they're rugged or clean?
>
>Can you, by just looking try to conclude,
>was this man gentle or mean?
>
>I'd like to share the hands of a man,
>and express just what they might tell.

This is about one who used his hands
to keep others from going to hell.

You see not everyone hears what is spoken today,
as their ears cannot pick up the sound

Of the Gospel as preached from churches around,
warning where people are bound.

We all at one time were bound for a place
that is dark and filled with pain.

Until we each realize and accept the fact
that Jesus for us he was slain.

So when I looked at the hands of my father today,
I saw scores of people gone by

Who through those hands were shared the truth,
and will now go to heaven when they die.

I earnestly pray that someday I too will have such a positive influence on others, hopefully through the sharing of this story.

Longest Ten Days of My Life

For ten days, from the night of his death to the time of the funeral, I wrestled in my mind with the mire I was dragging myself through. I was angry and frustrated from my decision to move from California in the first place. I was in a relationship that was totally out of the will of God. This became frighteningly obvious after Susan's comment, "Who is going to clean the backyard for the graduation party?" Susan and I were living together but not married, and she was of a different faith (unequally yoked). My job at the hotel was tormenting me, I was overwhelmed with frustration and anger because I was being used merely as a fix-it man, and from my being out of God's perfect will.

The week of Dad's home-going, there were several people staying at mom's house, and I was so preoccupied with the problems I had brought upon myself that I was in no mood to be around my brothers and others from the family. My position as a hotel general manager enabled me to secure a room for my cousin, so I decided to stay with him.

The ten days from Dad's death until his funeral were the longest ten days of my life. I was a mess.

Back to the Proverbial Pigpen

Upon my return to the proverbial pigpen, all these things combined brought on a bout with depression. One morning while shaving, I fainted and was taken to the hospital in an ambulance. Susan seemed more concerned about how my experience had scared her youngest child, who was about thirteen years old, than about my health. I was seen by the doctors, diagnosed with depression and anxiety, and given a prescription for Paxil and Ativan. However, after about a week of taking these medications, I was completely unable to stay awake at work, so I stopped taking them cold turkey.

This catapulted me head first into a suicidal state. One morning I pulled into the parking lot of the hotel where I worked. I just sat in my car looking at the bottles of Paxil and Ativan on the front seat, contemplating whether I should go into the hotel or just take all the pills right then. After sitting there for about half an hour, I called one of the other hotel managers, who came by to talk to me. After sharing some of the things going through my mind, I decided to admit myself into a mental health facility.

I went to a place that reminded me of the movie *One Flew Over the Cuckoo's Nest*. I was not allowed to have a belt or shoelaces; I was under constant surveillance, even in my own room. I would stand in line for them to give me whatever drugs they deemed necessary. I met with a psychiatrist each day. I was also given the opportunity to sit in group therapy, but I wasn't interested in that and contributed no feedback at all. After putting myself through all these self-inflicted problems, I continued to harbor "our little secret" in my heart, not sharing it with anyone.

I don't even think I made the connection between my childhood sexual abuse and what had become my lifestyle at this time. It's interesting to me that the psychiatrist, the counselors I had seen, nor anyone else was able to drag "our little secret" out of me.

After being at this facility for about ten days, my younger brother visited me. He works all over the country and had connections to make his way to see me. He suggested that I go and do some work around his house for him. He was doing some repairs and improvements, such as hanging doors and laying floors. I had gotten some experience doing both of those tasks while in the proverbial pigpen.

In a town not far away from my brother's house, I had done some training at a hotel that was a part of the management company. I remember swearing that I would never live in that area. The traffic was horrific, especially on the interstate, and I could not see ever putting myself through that on a regular basis.

This training had taken place about nine months prior to my brother making his suggestion. I decided to stay at my brother's house for a few weeks to work for him, and then I planned to continue on home to California.

Unbeknownst to him, my brother was a type of the father in the story of the prodigal son figuratively speaking, running out to meet and welcome him home. I checked myself out of the mental hospital, went back to the proverbial pigpen, and packed up to leave.

Susan and her kids were attending some event that kept them away for a couple of days, so while they were gone, I packed up everything I could fit into my little car. When they returned, I told her I was leaving. I couldn't believe she was actually surprised by my decision. There were some things that I couldn't fit in my car so they remain at the proverbial pigpen to this day.

Never Say Never

My brother had been very good to me, and things seemed to be going pretty well, but I needed to take care of some bills and other expenses, so after staying with him for about two months, I began looking for some supplemental income. After a rather short job search, I found a position and I started working for the same company where I had spent twenty-six years while living in California.

It's interesting to look back and see how God is always faithful to provide. I made the exact amount of money at this job, working a regular eight-hour schedule, as I had been making as a general manager in the hotel. As the general manager, I usually came in around 6:30 a.m. and was almost always there until at least 6:00 p.m., and sometimes as late as 10:00 p.m.

Nine months earlier, I resolved to never live in this area. I had heard before but learned from experience that you should never say never. Ironically, I eventually bought a house about a quarter of a mile from that same dreaded interstate.

The Proverbial Pigpen

I have recently been blessed to hear a series of messages on "The Far Country" taken from Luke Chapter 15. After consultation with my new pastor, I am including some of the outline with noted applications to my own personal experience in "the pigpen."

Nothing Is Too Much to Avoid the Proverbial Pigpen

What is the proverbial pigpen?

The proverbial pigpen is *any place* in your life where you don't want God to be. It is that part of your life where you have "Do Not Enter" signs, a place where you say to yourself, "God, you can't come here." I remember at times watching a movie and the language or other content would cause me to think to myself, "I'm glad my mom is not here." The fact is if I would be embarrassed or ashamed for my mom to see, hear, or experience something, I should be even more embarrassed and ashamed knowing that my omnipresent Father is there. If there are parts of your life where you do not want God to be, you have parts of your life where you don't want God to interfere, that is the proverbial pigpen.

Where is the proverbial pigpen?

When you go to the proverbial pigpen, you are also leaving somewhere. The prodigal son was *leaving* his father's house. When you go to the proverbial pigpen, wherever that may be, you are leaving God. Remember, God *never* leaves you, but you can move away from Him. When I went to the proverbial pigpen, I had left my home, my wife, her kids, a beautiful climate, and a good job, all in pursuit of a life that I knew was displeasing to God. Fortunately, I have many people in my life who continued to love and pray for me.

The eye-opening moment:

- An emerging of circumstances that have always been present but not addressed.

- When your experiences crash head first into God's Word while the power of the Holy Spirit subsequently changes your direction.

Too many times, we allow ourselves to be dragged down to the depths of despair before we come to an eye-opening moment. While reading the story of the prodigal son, one can observe that particular moment when he had this spiritual awakening:

> And when he came to himeself, he said, How many hired servents of my father's have bread enough to spare, and I perish with hunger! (Luke 15:17).

Realization that I am not where I need to be.

- Coming to grips with the fact that it is no one else's fault.
- Respond to the realization and return to God.

The Miry, Slippery Slope That Led to My Eye-Opening Moment

Realization: From a very young age, I knew something was not right, but I had neglected to face that realization myself, I continually struggled with being unable to "kick" this sin in my life.

Three Erroneous Ideas That May Cause You to Seek the Proverbial Pigpen

1. **I'm Missing Out on Life.**

    In search of freedom, some might say, there are too many boundaries, too many rules. God just takes all the fun out of life. The road to the proverbial pigpen is marked by wild living. Look at the prodigal son; he spent all his inheritance on riotous living. One might say, "God's path is just too narrow." People view the boundaries as fences to keep them from having a good time.

In retrospect, I found that my addiction, just like all other addictions, had me continually reaching for a bigger thrill, a higher high. Boundaries would prohibit me from reaching for those better things.

In actuality, the fences are there to protect us from enemies that might harm us or to keep us from falling over the edge of a dangerous cliff. Sin promises freedom but always delivers bondage, promises success but delivers failure, and promises life but brings death.

I was in desperate need of a guardrail to keep me from going off the edge. I neglected to take notice of the guardrails God had set in my life.

2. **God Just Doesn't Care.**

Some people view God as an impersonal force, not a loving, caring Father. One might consider: "Why did God allow this to happen to me?" "If God doesn't care about me, I'll just go do what I want." We are not required to understand Him but rather to trust Him. This idea stems from our own neglect to keep close to God through Bible reading and prayer. Our relationship with our kids or parents will be coupled with our view of our Heavenly Father.

3. **I Need Instant Gratification.**

The prodigal son wanted his father to give him his inheritance now; he didn't want to wait for his father to die. He had an insatiable craving to get his thrills now. He got what he thought he wanted, and then he lost it all.

My addiction had me to a point where, if I thought I wasn't

getting it often enough or fast enough or even good enough, I would turn to someone else for instant gratification. I learned one thing through it all: instant gratification is *never* lasting gratification; it is *always* very short-lived. We want God to do the same thing, give us stuff now! We don't want to wait for God's timing but rather pursue our own.

Later on in this book you'll read how Romans 8:28 is likened to baking a cake. We must learn to rely on God's timing, not our own.

The Ultimate Consequences of the Proverbial Pigpen

No matter what causes you to land in the proverbial pigpen, you will always discover that it is a place of desperation. At first it seems great, a wonderful time and a great feeling. The Bible shows us that there is pleasure in sin, *for a season* (Hebrews 11:25). People go to the far country to get away from their problems and, ironically, they find themselves in the proverbial pigpen.

I had eventually gotten to the point where I admitted myself into a mental health facility. I was out of my own answers and needed someone to rescue me from myself.

Every trip away from God ends the same way, in the proverbial pigpen. God-given talents are wasted away in the far country rather than being used to glorify God. A good job with a good income that could have been used to help send missionaries, support church planters, or fund programs in the church is wasted on instant gratification. He found himself in want and became a slave to the owner of the pigs. That's where this path away from God will eventually take you. True satisfaction never comes in the proverbial pigpen. You will always be seeking a new high. We must eventually come to understand that God *does* actually know what is best for us; we cannot outsmart Him.

> For my thoughts are not your thoughts, neither are your ways my ways, saith the Lord. For as the heavens are higher than the earth, so are my ways higher than your ways, and my thoughts than your thoughts. (Isaiah 55:8–9)

You must be completely realistic with yourself regarding your present status to avoid being drawn into the proverbial pigpen.

Some Things That Will Lead to an Eye-Opening Experience

1. Realization: Ignoring the Obvious Signs

What will it take for you to sit up and realize that you need a change? The effectiveness of any alarm is in direct correlation to how much you don't want to hear it. If the alarm has the soft sound of water running down a brook, you may ignore it and continue down the same road. If your alarm is the sound of a fire engine's siren or a blow horn, you will more promptly sit up and take notice. Only when the warning is so displeasurable that you can't take it anymore are you going to take the appropriate action to fix whatever it is that is wrong.

The realization occurs only when God finally gets our attention. What's it going to take this time? The warning comes, and it is so displeasurable that it causes us to take some kind of action. It causes us to realize that we are somewhere we shouldn't be, and we wonder, *How did I get here?* The prodigal son finally "came to himself ..." He woke up, he had his eye-opening experience. When you go down the road away from God, you never end up where you thought you were going.

The Prodigal Example

The warning came many times for the prodigal before he ended up in the pigpen. He didn't pay attention to it when he stood by his father and disrespectfully asked for his inheritance. He didn't pay heed to it staring him in the face when a few partying weekends caused him to run out of money. He didn't stand up and pay attention when the economy took a dive or when famine came to the land. He didn't even realize it when he took a job feeding pigs. It wasn't until he was ready to eat with the very pigs he was feeding that he realized where he had landed. How did he miss these warnings? The warnings were all around but were evidently not displeasurable enough.

What will it take for *you* to sit up and realize where you are?

My Personal Application

Looking back, I recall many such warnings in my head, and I simply ignored them.

- I had received counsel from a dear trusted and admired friend, but I didn't pay any attention; in essence, I just told him to mind his own business.
- I found myself engaging in websites that were inappropriate; I simply ignored that as a viable warning.
- When my wife, Geneva, threw my laptop across the living room, that should have been a signal to take note, that something was wrong, but I just continued down my road away from God.
- When I arrived in the proverbial pigpen and noticed that Susan had left the church of like faith, I should have stood up to take notice. I found myself in a church that was completely contrary to my beliefs, but I just didn't heed the warning.

I could go on and on with similar examples that were evidently just not displeasurable enough.

We have this idea that God only warns us when we hit rock bottom, that He waits for us to hit the bottom before coming to our aid. *Nothing* could be further from the truth.

> And the Lord God of their fathers sent to them by his messengers, rising up betimes, and sending; because he had compassion on his people, and on his dwelling place. (2 Chronicles 36:15)

God had been sending warnings by way of his messengers for two hundred years. He had compassion on his people, but the children of Israel just would not listen.

Three Sources of Warning That God Uses

A. The Bible.

The example of Cain and Abel: God had given Cain the opportunity to do the right thing and warned him that sin is crouching at the door. God has also given you the ability to refrain from whatever sin you may be struggling with; don't walk through that door. God uses His word to warn us of our errant ways.

> There hath no temptation taken you but such as is common to man: but God is faithful, who will not suffer you to be tempted above that ye are able; but will with the temptation also make a way to escape, that ye may be able to bear it. (1 Corinthians 10:13)

God had given pharaoh several opportunities to let the Children of Israel go, but he continually ignored the warnings, resulting in several plagues. Remember Lot's wife? There was ample warning given her, but she simply ignored the warning.

B.   The Word of Faithful, Godly Counsel.

The key here is *godly* counsel. Don't be looking for the counsel of soft words that tickle the ears, but rather seek out *honest*, godly counsel. Don't be wooed by those who are simply trying to make you feel okay. Seek counsel from someone who will be brutally honest, telling you what you *need* to hear and not just what you *want* to hear.

C.   Life Examples and Experiences.

God will use others who have traveled down their own roads away from him and have turned away from the warnings. If you pay attention, you can look to these examples so that you can avoid making the same mistakes. I believe we can also look to those who have continued to walk with God faithfully day in and day out. There are godly examples of how it *should* be done as well as how it shouldn't be done.

I can think of one particular bad example in my own life: A girl who was in my church got involved with drugs and became promiscuous and suffered greatly as a result. Had I been a little more observant and aware, this would have served as a warning for me.

I can also look to godly examples. Many men in my life have been stellar examples. I remember several Sunday school teachers, pastors and Bible college professors. I've been blessed to sit under good preaching, and I have seen the lives of evangelists who lived godly lives.

My father is another godly example. A poem I wrote for my father on Father's Day one year seems to hit the nail on the head.

Building Character

Dad, I wrote a poem for Mom on Mother's Day,
And everything in it is true.
So I thought, "What better way to express how I feel,
Than to write another, for you."

When I was a young teen I could sense you were trying
To build some character in me.
All the time you spent trying, you probably felt,
"Very little progress can I see."

But you did make an impact believe it or not,
And I'd like to express to you how.
It happened one day in a boat on the ocean,
You were astern and I was abow.

You see, halibut have to be twenty-two inches,
We were catching them and having a ball.
On one instance you caught one twenty-one and a quarter,
You looked at me and said, "I guess it's too small,"

Thank you, Dad for the way that you've tried,
To make my road smooth as could be.
The tragic part is, it seems too many times,
The bumps in the road I thought *I* should see.

There are many people in this big world,
And most are really quite nice.
But if I ever have questions or have any doubts,
It's to you, Dad, I'll go for advice.

We all need to continually pray that God will make us aware as we are given warnings, whether it be through our parents or other godly men and women. A close walk with God will give you a sensitive heart, receptive to the Holy Spirit and His direction. Remember, He will never leave you nor forsake you, but your actions can move you away from Him. Have a "Daily Devotion" that will keep you aware of God's desire for your life.

To conclude, the thought in 2 Chronicles 36:15 of God's alarms to the Children of Israel for over 200 years:

> But they mocked the messengers of God, and despised his words, and misused his prophets, until the wrath of the LORD arose against his people, till there was *no remedy*. (2 Chronicles 36:16, emphasis added)

2. Coming To Grips

The prodigal son came to a point when he had to come to grips with the facts. He could have denied the fact that he had landed in a pigpen, but that would not have altered the fact that he was indeed eating with the swine.

> And he would fain have filled his belly with the husks that the swine did eat: and no man gave unto him. And when he came to himself, he said, How many hired servants of my father's have bread enough and to spare, and I perish with hunger! (Luke 15:16–17)

When I was in my proverbial pigpen, I had to recognize that I had literally gone into a place that would eventually lead to total destruction. I had to come to a complete and honest reckoning. First of all, nothing that was happening to me was anybody else's fault but my own. Secondly, I had to be totally honest with myself, recognizing that if I did not get out of there, I would continue to be totally miserable.

God had allowed me to take myself to a point where suicidal thoughts were nearly ever-present. I had shamed Geneva, and I had shamed my parents and many others that I loved. I had also shamed myself to a point where I was seriously considering the option to simply check out. When I say God *allowed* me, I do not, in any sense of the word, imply that God forced any of this on me. I did *all* of this to myself.

3. Response

The prodigal son realized that he had come to a place where he was totally truthful with himself, and now he was at a crossroads in his life. He could either be content to eat with the swine, possibly out of shame of what his father and brother might think, or he could lay aside his pride, get up, and go back to his father's house. We know the story:

> And he arose, and came to his father. But when he was yet a great way off, his father saw him, and had compassion, and ran, and fell on his neck, and kissed him. And the son said unto him, Father, I have sinned against heaven, and in thy sight, and am no more worthy to be called thy son. (Luke 15:20–21)

I came to a painful realization, possibly at the point when Susan Boyles said, "You were going to clean the backyard for the graduation party." Whenever it took place, I became completely straightforward in my realization of where I had landed: the proverbial pigpen. I too had a decision to make. I could either be content in a miserable, ungodly setting—eating with the swine so to speak—or I could get up and do something about it.

When I was in the mental health facility and my brother came and convinced me to get out of the proverbial pigpen, I liken that to the father and his acceptance of my coming home. The shame I had brought upon myself, along with my pride, would have never allowed me to ask someone for help, especially one of my brothers. I know that sounds a bit askew, but that's what pride and shame can do to someone.

I did take the right road, and that week, I left the proverbial pigpen. I struggled for quite some time, but I did take the necessary action to remove myself from that ungodly environment.

I have done some evil and wicked things, but in each case, it was completely mutual between consenting adults. I just want to make it clear that not all sexually abused children turn into child abusers. The fact is that most do not. There are references in the back of this book that will help in understanding some of the effects related to men who were sexually abused as children. I encourage you to read and examine these references carefully.

There *is* redemption from even the vilest things that one could do. Only by the grace of a loving God have I been able to receive forgiveness.

> But by the grace of God I am what I am: and His grace which was bestowed upon me was not in vain. (1 Corinthians 15:10)

Thank you, Lord.

Chapter 5

Home Run

After making the move from the proverbial pigpen, I was still suffering from a lot of anxiety, depression, and pain. I had lost the best friend I'd ever had in my father. As I look back, during a time when I could have used some good godly counsel and support after the loss of my father, I had alienated my long-time valued advisor Dr. Landon. I had made a total shambles of my life, doing things I knew were displeasing to God, my mother, and my friends. The general labor I was doing for my brother was helping me get my mind off some of these things, but I was still a basket case.

I joined a local church some of my California friends were attending, and eventually I got involved with singing in the choir and teaching a junior high Sunday school class. I attended this church for almost ten years. I remember, after being there for about nine years, a lady at our church commented on how much I had changed. She had noticed when I first began going to that church how much pain I was experiencing. Little did she know, I still had "our little secret" that had not yet been revealed.

After a short time, I followed my usual path and once again began looking for companionship, in part to help ease my pain. I dated several ladies but never seemed to find a fit. Then, after

OUR LITTLE SECRET, REVEALED

about three years, while looking through a dating website, I became acquainted with Sabrina. Her dating site profile read something like this: "Likes to fish and golf."

I responded to her ad simply: "Fish *and* Golf? ...Wow!" We corresponded through the website for a couple weeks until, one day, she invited me to come to her apartment. I immediately jumped in the car and made the 25- to 30-mile drive to see her.

I distinctly remember one thing from when I walked into her apartment: the first thing I saw was the shotgun she had in the living room. I also saw a brick that had been broken in half and had some writing on it. I learned that she was a second-degree black belt in Tae Kwon Do. *I'd better mind my p's and q's with this one,* I thought. After our initial meeting there were very few days when we didn't see each other, and literally *no* days when we didn't at least talk to one another on the phone.

I remember once, when Sabrina was on vacation with her family at South Padre Island and I was at my family reunion in Colorado, and I called her to get advice on a price for jalapeño jelly that was being sold at our family reunion auction. That was just an excuse to call her. *Yep, this has* got *to be it,* I thought.

I had been instantly attracted to Sabrina's joyful personality and her unbelievable ability to stay positive. After a few weeks, she came with me to church, and everyone fell in love with her, and especially her laugh! She continued to come to church with me and eventually accepted Jesus Christ as her personal savior. Interestingly and in God's providence, the lady who led Sabrina to Christ was Cathy, the daughter of Mrs. Sanger ... that's the lady who knocked on my door when I was seven and invited me to DVBS.

I couldn't help but think to myself, *I have finally kicked this thing, she is definitely* the one! After a rather short time, I asked Sabrina to marry me, and she said yes, and the date was set! Sabrina and I were married and began serving in our church.

She sang with me in the choir and came in as my secretary in the junior high Sunday school class.

About six weeks after our wedding, Sabrina was diagnosed with breast cancer. Displaying an incredibly positive attitude, Sabrina faced this challenge head-on. After chemotherapy, radiation, and several surgeries, she came through it all like the champ she is, and we drew closer to each other through that trial.

Going back to my thought that I had finally kicked this thing, and that she was *the one*, I was correct in one part: she is definitely the one. However, after five years of marriage, history repeated itself. *Why can't I get control of this thing?* I kept thinking. I seemed to never be satisfied.

Sabrina discovered that I had been looking in the personal ads on another website and that I had responded to a woman's advertisement. While it is true that I did reply to the ad, I had never gone to meet her. Mainly because, contrary to what they might say, the women on those sites are almost always looking for monetary compensation, and I wasn't going to pay. Somehow it seems I had rationalized in my mind that I wasn't going to give my "mission money" for this purpose. You can see how twisted my thought process was.

I stuck to my story. She persisted that I had to have met this woman, and I continued to deny it. "Someone hacked into my email, social media, or something," I argued. We finally decided that we should seek counseling from our pastor. Although this counseling did address and help some of our issues, it also reinforced to Sabrina that I was not being totally honest with her. The warning was once again obvious as God kept trying to get my attention. I was again heading down a road to a place where God didn't want me to be, another proverbial pig pen; I was clearly not in His perfect will.

I continued to reject her accusations that I had met this woman until she finally gave me an ultimatum. The text message read something like this: "You are not being completely honest with me. I can live with just about anything you may have done, but I cannot live with this dishonesty. Just let me know when you want me out of your house and I'm gone."

Here is another realization as I finally understood that I had to come clean. If I didn't tell her the whole truth, she would leave; if I did tell her the whole truth, she might leave anyway. I texted back to her that I would come completely clean with her if she would be willing to listen. Sabrina agreed.

The Cat's Out of the Bag ... "Our Little Secret—Revealed"

When Sabrina came home from work that evening I told her that I was indeed being honest in that I'd never met the woman from the ad. I then told her that the reason was because these women wanted money, and I wasn't going to pay. I then told her that, although I had never hooked up with that woman, I did seek out and found a man in town who was willing and even wanted to give me instant gratification.

As a part of yet another eye-opening moment, I had to be completely honest to get through another pigpen experience. After having concealed my deep secret for more than fifty-five years, it had finally become "our little secret—revealed." It was as though God brought back to the forefront of my mind the experiences I'd had with my uncle.

I shared with Sabrina that when I was a little boy, my uncle had coerced me into a hiding place and he began fondling and touching me in an inappropriate way. "My uncle sexually abused me when I was a little boy," I told her. I had considered that she might simply get up and walk out, but Sabrina wrapped her arms around me and showed her unbelievable love and support. She showed her willingness and compassion to deal with the process of healing from a secret I had suppressed for over half a century.

Sabrina confirmed that she was going to help me get through this ordeal. After I had truly come *completely* clean, I experienced an unbelievable sense of relief, and a particular scripture came to mind. I have heard this verse many times, but it always has so much more meaning when it becomes applicable in your own life. It was at that point that the verse came alive to me. I finally felt totally free from the weight of that sin.

> And ye shall know the truth, and the truth shall make you free. (John 8:32)

I have a rather crude analogy to express this feeling. Don't worry, if the things I have shared haven't completely disgusted you to this point, rest assured this analogy will not be any more disgusting. I was imagining a scenario in which one could be seriously constipated for several months, and then finally the needed relief comes. My life was completely bloated with filth and impurity that had built up over fifty-five years, and then I experienced an unbelievable sense of relief.

I shared this analogy with a friend, and he referred to it as a "spiritual enema." I was completely cleaned out. The truth has indeed set me free.

No Claim to Be a Doctor

Since the age of about eight I had experienced episodes of fainting. The first one I remember was when I was getting blood drawn, so it was naturally written off as "white coat syndrome" caused by visits to the doctor's office. Through the years, I have repeatedly had these episodes, and most times it was in fact while having something done at a doctor's office, e.g., blood tests, stitches, and even simply getting a shot.

A few years ago, I was just sitting at the dining room table with Sabrina and I took a sip of my iced tea. I became light-headed. I took another sip, and she could tell something was wrong. I told her that I just wanted to go lie down in my bed. She insisted that

OUR LITTLE SECRET, REVEALED

I sit there for a few minutes, but eventually, Sabrina agreed to let me go to the bedroom.

I remember taking about two steps, and then I woke up about fifteen steps farther, in the computer room. I had not been to the doctor's office recently, and I just couldn't figure out what had happened, but I passed out cold. When I was waking up, Sabrina asked me, "Do you know where you are?" I put my hands down to my sides, felt the floor, and then responded, "I know I'm not in my bed." Since that episode, I have had an MRI, CT scan, EEG, EKG, and a bunch of other acronyms, only to find nothing wrong.

Since my undisclosed lifestyle had become "our little secret—revealed," I have had a lot fewer feelings of light-headedness and have not passed out once. I'm not a doctor, but I have come to the logical speculation that these episodes could have been a stress-related condition. I can honestly say that I feel better than I have in years, and possibly in all my life. I have been able to release the stress; I've gotten my life in line with what God wants, and my emotional condition has improved drastically.

No words can express how grateful and thankful I am to Sabrina, who could have understandably taken a much easier (and unfortunately much more traveled) road out. When all this happened, I couldn't help but ponder, *All things work together for good*. I had heard and even quoted this to others and had, on a surface level, believed it, but I could not imagine how in the world any good could come from "our little secret— revealed."

Five years earlier, we had quoted this same scripture when Sabrina had been diagnosed with breast cancer. Ironically, she likened the support I was able to provide for her during *our* fight with cancer to that of her now being able to help me through this, *our* healing process.

Still in the Proverbial Pigpen—Time for a Realization. As Sabrina and I shared "our little secret—revealed" with our pastor, he gave us both a book to read, *Breaking the Bondage of Addictions*. I took that book with me to work that night and began reading;

then I came to a point where it mentioned a word that I had heard and been familiar with all my life: *repent!* It was then that it hit me like a brick ... when I was twelve years old, I got my "fire insurance." At that time, I had gone through all four steps of the Roman's Road:

1. Realize you are a sinner. For all have sinned, and come short of the glory of God; (Romans 3:23).
2. Realize that there is a penalty for our sin. For the wages of sin is death; (Romans 6:23a).
3. Realize that God made that payment through His son, Jesus Christ. But God commendeth His love toward us, in that, while we were yet sinners, Christ died for us. (Romans 5:8).
4. Receive this free gift of salvation. That if thou shalt confess with thy mouth the Lord Jesus, and shalt believe in thine heart that God hath raised Him from the dead, thou shalt be saved. For with the heart man believeth unto righteousness; and with the mouth confession is made unto salvation. For whosoever shall call upon the name of the Lord shall be saved. (Romans 10:9-10, 13)

I had even prayed "the sinner's prayer," but I had never genuinely repented.

Repent: to turn from sin and dedicate oneself to the amendment of one's life.

I told my coworker that I was going home for "lunch." I called Sabrina at about 3:00 that morning and told her I was on my way home for my lunch break. While I was driving, I thought to myself, *This is it!* I was so excited to finally get this nailed down. I was actually repenting and accepting Christ on my way home as

I thought to myself, *What if I get in an accident before I get home?* God knew my heart.

When I arrived at home, we sat at the dining room table with my Bible, and I asked Sabrina if she could show me how to be saved. After a look of complete bewilderment on her face, we both took the Bible and walked down the Roman's Road. Refer to previous examples of the Roman's Road.

Something's Missing

I then asked Sabrina, "What's missing?" She didn't quite understand what I was asking so I pointed out to her, "There is nothing in there about *repentance*." I had gone to church and heard enough preaching to know that this was a vital part of the salvation process.

> Then Peter said unto them, *Repent* and be baptized every one of you in the name of Jesus Christ for the remission of sins, and ye shall receive the gift of the Holy Ghost. (Acts 2:38, emphasis added)
> I tell you, Nay: but, except ye *repent*, ye shall all likewise perish. (Luke 13:3, emphasis added)

Response: I then bowed my head and confessed to God that I had never repented. Right there in the dining room of my home on May 6, 2016, at 3:30 in the morning, I nailed it down once and for all. I received the free gift of salvation. Just like the prodigal son's father was waiting for him to come home, God the Father was waiting with open arms to welcome me into His family. I have turned around and forsaken "our little secret—revealed" and am now on my way to a healthy, God-centered relationship and a God-glorifying life.

Get Hook'd On Jesus

Prior to nailing down my salvation, I had started my own ministry, which I called "Get Hook'd on Jesus." I developed a Gospel tract with the same title that I have used while fishing at the pond or lake. When I first designed the tract, it had the Romans Road as the way to salvation, but since my conversion, I've added verses to include the need for repentance.

Several years ago, I began making my own lures to fish for largemouth bass. The lure is a floating "popper" that is used on the surface to catch the bass. On one side of the lures, I have inscribed my name, and on the other side the reference:

> And he saith unto them, follow me and I will make you fishers of men. (Matthew 4:19)

I use these lures as a way to break the ice with other fishermen. I give the lures away along with the Gospel tract, and then I witness and invite them to attend my church. I believe we should use any creative means possible to reach others for the cause of Jesus Christ.

All Things ...

Not long after Sabrina found me out, she shared our experience with another couple. This led to a revelation that they were experiencing a similar struggle with the husband's battle with drug abuse. Since then, we have been able to work with each other and have made great strides in this healing process. Once again, I have to consider:

> And we know that *all things* work together for
> good to them that love God, to them who are the

called according to his purpose. (Romans 8:28, emphasis added)

The simple act of sharing your experience could be of great help and comfort to others who may be experiencing similar struggles.

I have begun a process to reunite with my children, as we haven't spoken to each other since the death of my father ten years ago. I have been corresponding with the younger one via messenger and, just recently, we spoke for nearly half an hour. I shared "our little secret—revealed," and it was received with an open mind. It was the first time we had spoken to each other in nine years.

The passing of my mom's sister had given me cause to return to California. I arrived on Saturday morning, and that evening, my daughter came over to my mom's house and I was introduced to her husband. It was the first time we had met, and we all had a great reunion. This is just one example of how, in due time, "all things work together for good."

After sharing my story in my Bible class, I learned that one of the young ladies in our class, while she was not struggling with addictions, was unsure of her salvation. I shared this story (not in detail), and as a result, she settled her doubts also.

After being given the book *Breaking the Bondage of Addictions*, by Mike Keller, I nailed down my own salvation. After one *truly* accepts Jesus Christ and His free gift, he cannot contain himself. Such was the case with me. I called my dear friend Dr. Landon and shared my story with him (refer to chapter 4). He rejoiced with me and shared the name of someone named Rick Blue who could help me. Rick Blue is the author of the book *Easy Living: Living the Lord's Prayer*. I have since met with Rick, and he shared some of his story with me. He gave me a copy of his book, and I read it as soon as I got home. Once you begin applying the truths that are shared in this book, along with other good Christian publications, you will be able to make great strides in the healing process.

Another factor playing into my decision to write my story was the testimony of Rick Blue. Rick told me of an instance where he was addressing a class of men students at a Bible college explaining his experience with sexual abuse. At the end of his presentation he told the class that if anyone had questions or just wanted to talk that his door would be open. Rick shared with me that ten minutes after the class was dismissed, there was a line of students outside his office.

This example simply reinforces to me the need to share with others experiences that many men have had and it's generally a secret.

In one of the sessions with our pastor I expressed a concern that, in the future my wife might pull something from my past out of her memory and continue to hold it over my head. We agreed that night to figuratively draw a line in the sand setting that date as the new beginning.

Sabrina and I had determined that God was calling us to be of help, not only to those abused but also to others affected by such abuse. It seems I've been getting all the attention in the process of healing, but my wife has also come through a horrific experience and needs direction. We had committed to be available for God to use us in that capacity.

Roller Coaster Ride

Over a period of approximately 2 years some things had happened to continue putting us to the test. About 5 months after nailing down my salvation I was laid off my job. The company would continue paying me from October of 2016 through the middle of February 2017. I turned 62 earlier in February so I decided to file for Social Security. Sabrina had also been laid off so we decided to put our house up for sale and move about

60 miles north to be with Sabrina's daughter, son in law and the grand daughters. The original plan here was to use the money from the sale of the house to purchase another house somewhere near the kids.

One thing Sabrina and I had agreed on was regarding my text messages. Whenever I received a text, phone call, email or any other message I would inform Sabrina prior to deleting the message. This agreement was going well as a method of accountability. It had gotten to where when I received a text message I would show her from across the room and she would respond yeah yeah okay delete it. It had become a rather informal process.

One day I was applying for a part time job and came to a place where they were asking for the phone number of my previous employer. I no longer had that number in my phone but knew someone that I worked with who would have it because her husband still worked at that company. I sent a message asking for the phone number and within a few minutes a response came. I input the phone number into the application and then, without even thinking about it, deleted the number.

A few minutes later Sabrina called asking for the number of my previous employer. She had been making inquiries about getting pre-approved to buy a house. I told her that I just got it but deleted it. "You what?" She exclaimed.

When she got home she insisted that we separate and asked me to leave. I stayed for a couple more nights then started making plans to leave. I had a very hard time believing that this simple breach would cause such turmoil. That being said, I still take full responsibility as it was a violation of our agreement.

I have to again wonder how this could all be working for good but I have given it to God and trust that His will is being done.

I was obviously distraught about the whole thing and decided to get away in an effort to start over. I knew that my Social Security would not support me in the metroplex area where I was living so I moved about 300 miles north to a small town in Kansas. I knew that the cost of living would be more doable there and I could get a new start.

I stayed with my uncle for a couple weeks then found a place to move. After securing the apartment and getting a car, I made a trip to California to spend time with my mom. After about a month I made the trip back to my apartment.

When I first moved here I again felt the need to find some companionship to satisify my physical desires. For a short time I was searching on the personals for such encounters. One day I finally came to realize that I was more concerned about what Sabrina might think, and that *she* would find out rather than what God thinks. I then made the commitment to put God first in everything.

One day while watching a movie there was a point where someone said something and I thought to myself, if my mom was watching this with me I'd be embarrassed. It then occurred to me that while mom is not here, Jesus is as he lives within me.

One day after hearing my pastor preach on getting the leaven out (referring to all the things that might be displeasing to God), I began to do an inventory and began to clean out my apartment removing any DVD's that would be construed as inappropriate and have made my apartment a place where Jesus would be welcome, after all… He does live there with me. I have since noticed that I've become a lot more sensitive to things that used to be no big deal. Some people may think I'm a little crazy because I'll be walking around the apartment talking to Jesus.

I think of all these things that have come to pass as a result of Sabrina "finding me out." Because of her burden, desire, and persistence to confront me with it, I continue to consider the significance of this verse:

> And we know that *all things* work together for
> good to them that love God, to them who are the

called according to His purpose. (Romans 8:28, emphasis added)

For example:

- My salvation has become my Home Run.
- A couple where the husband was dealing with drug addiction.
- Reuniting with one of my children, another Home Run.
- Reuniting with my dear friend, Dr. Landon.
- A lady, who heard my story, nailed down her own salvation.
- I've established a consistent daily devotion to establish a closer relationship with God.
- My experience of healing and dealing with the effects of the sexual abuse, such as anger and issues with intimacy.

And again I say ... *all things!*

Don't Allow Yourself to Get "Fired"

Many people think that once you get married, it is like a magic wand has been waved over your heads, causing you to live happily ever after. Nothing could be further from the truth. Although marriage is not like a business endeavor, I do believe that anyone contemplating this giant step of a lifetime relationship should take the effort to follow a strategic plan:

First, if you are a Christian, you should have *no* aspirations to marry or even date anyone who is not a Christian.

> Be ye not unequally yoked together with unbelievers: for what fellowship hath righteousness with unrighteousness? And what communion hath light with darkness? (2 Corinthians 6:14)

This verse draws a parallel about two people trying to go in one direction yet being "yoked" with someone of a different viewpoint. Imagine a team of oxen attempting to go in different directions. This would cause the yoke to rub upon the back of the neck, causing sores and calluses; they are unequally yoked.

- Marriage is hard enough without having an unequally yoked mate causing such irritations.
- Consider your thoughts on having children. While she may want six, he may only want two ... or none.
- The best way to avoid any such relationship is to not even date one who is not of your belief.

After determining that you are both of the same mind, spiritually speaking, you should talk about your lifetime goals. This is something that both parties should prayerfully consider. Don't wait until your fifth anniversary to discuss what God's plan for your life may be.

- Frustration and irritation is imminent, and even more so if you are both headed in different directions.
- If one of you has every intention of being a missionary to a foreign country and the other has no desire to leave America, that may (probably *will*) be a problem.

Take into serious consideration the love verses in 1 Corinthians 13. These verses give a very good biblical definition of what love is ... and is not.

> [4]Charity suffereth long, and is kind; charity envieth not; charity vaunteth not itself, is not puffed up, [5]Doth not behave itself unseemly, seeketh not her own, is not easily provoked, thinketh no evil; [6]Rejoiceth not in iniquity, but

rejoiceth in the truth; ⁷Beareth all things, believeth all things, hopeth all things, endureth all things. (1 Corinthians 13:4–7)

The word *charity* here can be interpreted as "agape love," or love that is unconditional. This scripture should be studied not just to see if you think *you* are in love, but also (and probably just as importantly) for you each to see if you really believe your mate truly loves you. For example:

- You may think you are measuring up to these characteristics; however, your mate may see things in a different light. Take verse 4, for example: "Charity suffereth long …" You may think you've been patient. "Why can't I get a kiss? After all we've been dating for three weeks now?"
- Your mate might not feel it is the time yet and that those things can wait. Your mate is willing to practice "Charity suffereth long …" This would more seriously be applicable as it would pertain to any pre-marital sexual encounters, not limited to intercourse only.
- Marriage should never be approached simply as an opportunity for guilt-free sex. My own experience truly bears this out.

Total honesty is critical. Few things are more devastating to a marriage than to find out secrets after you've been married for several years.

The single most important thing to my wife was to be assured that I was being completely honest with her. Because of the nature of "our little secret," not yet revealed, I felt she would not understand, and I would be risking our marriage if I were to be totally honest with her. (Remember, one of the ramifications of those affected by sexual abuse as a child is being unable to trust.)

I could not trust that Sabrina would understand my dilemma. Thankfully, she persisted and convinced me that she could deal with just about anything ... except dishonesty. When I finally came to the conclusion that it was either come clean or she would leave, I became totally honest with her.

This is something that should not only be brought out at the beginning of a relationship, but also throughout the relationship.

As I had previously mentioned, Sabrina and I have an agreement that whenever I receive a text message and it poses any questions, we both look at it and, generally without opening it, we delete it together. This may sound a little like overkill, but remember: you don't want there to be even an appearance of impropriety. "Abstain from all appearance of evil" (1 Thessalonians 5:22).

- It's interesting that Paul doesn't write that we should abstain from all evil, but rather all *appearance* of evil.
- It may be that those text messages mean nothing, but if it causes an *appearance* of evil, you don't want to plant those seeds of doubt into the mind of your mate.

Marriage is not an easy undertaking even under the most ideal circumstances. Remember, the devil wants your marriage to fail. Marriage is the very first institution that God ordained, even before the church, and God's desire is that it remain unbroken and thriving.

Consider this thought-provoking question: if you got a job and paid as much attention to the success of your career through that job as you do to your wife and your marriage, would you still be employed?

Don't let it get to the point where your mate has to make the decision to fire you from your marriage.

I've been fired

Unfortunately for me, Sabrina's decision for us has escalated, or rather de-escalated to the filing for a divorce. I have made drastic changes in my life as a result of our little secret being revealed. No matter how much you get your life in order, there are natural consequences of sin and I am experiencing those consequences now. These consequences are merely distasteful ingredients to God's perfect will for my life.

You might be asking yourself, "how can you be giving me advice on marriage, after all you've been married three times?"

I can completely understand that question and can only use a comment I learned from my father. My dad might be doing something around the house and it wouldn't turn out right, his comment to me was, "son, that's how *not* to do it". You would be completely right about my disqualifications as a marriage counselor but I *can* tell you how *not* to do it.

Remember when I was managing a hotel on the central coast of California and went to the proverbial pig pen? The pain I had caused my wife, her kids, my kids and many others, I am now reaping the consequences.

I currently live in a very small town in rural Kansas. I have found a good church and am closer to God than I've ever been but my heart still aches. I still love Sabrina with all my heart and the idea of never reconciling pains me deeply. This all may sound like an ugly end to what could have been a beautiful story but the results of sin are devastating in every way.

I have turned it all over to God, if He desires to perform a miracle and reconcile Sabrina and me, so be it. Either way, God has now taken total preeminence in my life. As I continue on, I really don't foresee any relationships in the future but only God knows the answer to that mystery.

Chapter 6

Brand New Ball Game

Get God Off the Bench

One of the ways I've begun my healing process is to discuss with others who have had in the past, or are currently having, similar experiences. Some good authors have written books on how to live one day at a time. One in particular uses The Lord's Prayer as a model, not for praying, but rather for *living* a life of victory over any sin that may easily beset you. I strongly encourage you to find some good Christian-based books that deal specifically with this subject. Refer to the bibliography at the back of this book for some ideas.

    I have heard since my youth that we should have a daily devotion for ourselves. I do believe that it is important, but I am sometimes hard-headed and need a brick to hit me (figuratively speaking). I had heard of a Daily Devotional pamphlet called: *Our Daily Bread* for many years. My mother, in fact, turns to it every day and has for years. I had never even so much as picked it up until all this came about in my life.

    I always tried to do my devotions by simply finding a scripture to read, racing through it, and then brushing my hands off—"There, done for today!" A daily devotion to me was always the chore of reading (something I've never really enjoyed) a lot more than I really wanted and then trying to apply what I had read to my own self-centered life.

I have found that publications such as *Our Daily Bread* are very helpful in developing a consistent, regular schedule designed to help you take some kind of action when it comes to a daily devotion. *Our Daily Bread* is short and concise, but it's geared to an action based on the scripture for the day. Because it is not lengthy, one is more likely to make a daily practice of reading it.

I just thought of another analogy. I have been a baseball fan all my life, and one of my favorite baseball movies is *The Natural*. I remember when Roy Hobbs, portrayed by Robert Redford, first joined the Knights; the manager wouldn't allow Roy to play because, in the words of the manager, "we don't need any middle-aged rookies."

The Knights were on a terrible losing streak when finally, one day the manager allowed Roy Hobbs to hit during batting practice, at which time he hit every ball out of the park. Roy Hobbs's talent had been totally wasted because the manager refused to put him in the game. Once he began to use the resource (Roy Hobbs) available to him, the Knights were nearly unbeatable.

Not having daily devotions is like keeping God on the bench. Because we are Christians, He is on our roster as an available resource, but if the most valuable and treasured resource you have is kept out of the game, He is of little help. It's time now to get God off the bench and let Him go to bat for you ... daily!

Preventive Maintenance

I have talked to several people about my experience as a victim of child sexual abuse. Without exception, everyone who has had a similar experience has also suffered many of the consequences of such abuse that I have mentioned before.

Victory over any addiction starts with an understanding that you can't overcome the addiction by yourself. Studies show that about 50 percent of the victory with any addiction is simply admitting that you have the addiction (or any other problem).

Admit:

- I have a problem, an addiction.
- I cannot get victory over this addiction on my own.

Acknowledge:

- The same God who created me is able to fix me.

We need to follow the operations manual for life—the Holy Bible. If we do our daily maintenance, we can avoid a lot of the catastrophic problems we bring upon ourselves.

My father was a Customer Engineer for a computer company, and one of his responsibilities was to perform PMs on different kinds of equipment. PM is a preventive maintenance plan to ensure the equipment is in proper working condition, much like getting a tune-up, oil change, or any other scheduled service for your car.

I believe one reason people have a hard time reading the Bible regularly is because it points out our shortcomings, and no one likes to hear about their shortcomings. But in the same way that we need to know when something is wrong with our car, we need to know when *we* need something fixed even more so.

> For the word of God is quick, and powerful, and sharper than any two-edged sword, piercing even to the dividing asunder of soul and spirit, and of

the joints and marrow, and is a discerner of the thoughts and intents of the heart. (Hebrews 4:12)

In this day and age, it seems the goal of our educators is not necessarily to teach, but rather to give students a sense of self-worth. Ironically, if the students actually learn, they will in turn be less likely to have low self-esteem. We need to know where we fall short so we can ask the Holy Spirit to guide us accordingly.

I have a manual for my air conditioner at home, and I really don't like to open and read it, because I will find all the things I should be doing to maintain the equipment. If I neglect the needed service, I will inevitably pay for my neglect. How much more important it is to take care of our spiritual PMs.

I have started using *Our Daily Bread* as a type of daily preventive maintenance to ensure I keep my spiritual life in good working condition.

The Bible shows us that we are in a race, and we should do all we can to win that race:

> Wherefore seeing we also are compassed about with so great a cloud of witnesses, let us lay aside every weight, and the sin which doth so easily beset us, and let us run with patience the race that is set before us, Looking unto Jesus the author and finisher of our faith; who for the joy that was set before him endured the cross, despising the shame, and is set down at the right hand of the throne of God. (Hebrews 12:1–2)

"Every weight" does not necessarily refer to sins but rather to anything that hinders us from doing our best for God. I ran track in high school and remember stripping down to the bare minimum in order to be as weight-free as possible. It's hard to run a race of any kind with weights hanging around your neck.

One Day at a Time

Since starting to regularly read and meditate on *Our Daily Bread*, I have found myself sometimes trying to foresee the future by reading tomorrow's *Daily Bread* today. It seems ironic ... the very thing I had so much trouble with, reading, seems to be a joy now rather than a chore. When I was working, because of my work schedule, I was usually awake right at midnight, and I could hardly wait for midnight to roll around so I could find out what was in store for me the next day.

But when I feel the urge to read ahead, I recall what God told Moses in the wilderness when He provided manna on a daily basis: *only* take enough for today. While I am excited to see what's in the making for my tomorrow, we should have a devotion of some kind, from day to day.

It is very difficult to practice "Give us this day our *daily* bread ..." when we don't do our *daily* devotions. I believe the important thing is to be consistent in your devotions. Trying to read a lengthy passage of scripture, dissect it, and then apply it to your daily life can be overwhelming at first. As you begin with a simple daily devotion, such as *Our Daily Bread,* and become consistent in practicing it every day, you will naturally grow in knowledge and in truth. You will therefore increase your *desire* to spend more time reading the word of God.

I have since found other publications, like *Loved Beyond Measure* and *Call to Glory,* available through my new church. It seems I no longer look at daily devotions as a chore but an opportunity to see what God has for me on a daily basis.

I'm taking other systematic steps. For instance, I read Proverbs, one a day based on the day of the month. For example, on the first of the month, I'll read Proverbs 1; on the second day of the month, Proverbs 2; and so on. You can also choose a subject matter, such as a study of the Tabernacle or a study of the Gospels. I started to do a Bible reading on all the letters that the Apostle Paul wrote. Also the books of poetry, prophets, etc.

Have a Cup of Coffee with God

At a recent family reunion, I was sharing my struggles with developing a daily devotion. One of my cousins told me about his solution in regards to his daily time with God. He told me that he used to go to the coffee shop or simply sit at the dining room table and open the daily newspaper to read while he drank his morning coffee. He came to realize that he was spending more time on the morning newspaper than he was with God. He began taking his Bible with him to the coffee shop or at the dining room table and would spend that time having "a cup of coffee with God."

Rather than starting the day with all the negative things you're bound to read in the newspaper, have a cup of coffee with God. This is a good way to make effective strides toward a meaningful daily devotion.

Attainable Goals Result in Consistency

When I was a manager, I would try to set goals for my staff that were *attainable*. You should do the same with your daily devotion. If you have never read a single chapter from the Bible in a day, it might not be a good idea to set a goal of reading four chapters a day, as some plans suggest for reading through the Bible in a year.

Consistency is the key. Take small steps and grow as you develop in your Christian walk. Possibly set a goal to read the Old Testament one year, and then the New Testament. After setting and meeting goals that are attainable, you will find that your daily time with God will become more enjoyable, and subsequently, you'll have a consistent daily walk with God. Unattainable, unrealistic goals only lead to frustration, and eventually you'll stop trying.

Share your story. It is not necessary to elaborate on all the horrific details, but going through any life-altering ordeal like this and coming out victorious in the end can be a powerful testimony. You will be amazed how many others are struggling with very similar experiences. There is no other explanation regarding how I have made it this far except for the grace of God. I have a completely new and clearer appreciation of what Paul meant when he wrote: "*all* things work together for good."

There Is No Magic Potion

In virtually every case such as my experience, someone has been hurt. There is no magic word or some special formula you can take or give someone that will make the hurt go away. I remember as a youngster, when one of us boys would scrape a knee or something, my father would break into song with an old Ames Brother's tune, "It Only Hurts for a Little While."

The challenge you are facing is that of rebuilding trust that has been broken and compromised. It will take a lot of work and may be a very lengthy process. Some wounds don't "only hurt for a little while" but need some timely, extensive healing to take place.

My deepest desire, if it were possible, would be to erase all the pain and distrust I have caused so many people, but it just doesn't happen that way. I believe deep in my heart that I have now, by the grace of God and only with His help, kicked this thing. However, there is still a lot of healing to be done, both for me and for all who have been hurt as a result of this ordeal. Remember, all things work together for good, not just for you, but for the ones you've hurt, also.

Discretion

I have found that even when I am genuinely attempting to help others who may have experienced similar issues, I must be sensitive to the feelings of distrust that I have planted in my wife. While a genuine attempt to help others may have all good intentions, if it stirs up my wife's feelings of mistrust, then the whole thing becomes a moot point, as the very one I initially hurt now has scabs of the wound ripped away, causing recurring pain. Here are a few things that may help you avoid such setbacks:

- Do whatever it takes to regain lost trust.
    - One suggestion made to me was to let my wife take complete control of my phone whenever she wants.
    - Allow your spouse to monitor your phone calls, your text messages, social media, email, or any other means whereby you could have potential secrets.
    - This will force you to be accountable to the very one you have ultimately hurt, and if you are serious about restoring a lost trust, this will produce valuable strides to that end. *Force* may sound like a drastic step, but remember; this is not her fault.
- Don't blame your spouse for the mess you have caused.
    - "Well, I would never have done this if you hadn't (or had)" fill-in-the-blank.
    - While it is true that these actions may stem from a sexually abusive situation as a child, you still must take it upon yourself as an adult to own up to this as your problem.
    - Your spouse has been devastated by the very one who has promised to love and care for her. Your actions, *not hers*, have caused this problem.

- All the steps you take to re-gain the broken trust may or may not result in restitution. I am trusting God to direct me going forward.
- Make amends to those you have hurt (if possible).

When I was young, my mother would come into my room, and one of her frequent comments was, "This room looks like a hurricane hit it." Her point was that it looked like a path of destruction a hurricane or tornado might leave behind.

Through my life's path of destruction (possibly like that of a category 5 hurricane), I have hurt many people. There are some that I don't even know how to contact to make amends, but there are also some that I should make no attempt to contact.

Remember, the focus here is to regain trust with your spouse. Any attempt to contact someone from your past may (and probably will) only cause more feelings of distrust in your spouse. This was, in fact, my modus operandi as observed by Sabrina. However genuine your motives may be, it will still appear to be history repeating itself. Remember: "abstain from all appearance of evil" (1 Thessalonians 5:22).

If there are grown children involved, it would be a wonderful thing to restore a relationship. Relationships can be restored between children and stepchildren alike.

Ex-spouses and former partners have, in my case, been so deeply hurt that the last thing they want is for me to try restoration of any kind. This would also most likely create a big question mark in the mind of my wife.

In some cases, the ex may be remarried or in a new relationship, and any contact may simply cause more problems in *their* new life, and that should not be the goal here.

One important objective here is forgiveness ... both

asking for your needed forgiveness and also forgiving others.

In the case of those you probably shouldn't contact, talk to God. He knows your heart and can perform a miracle in your life and in the lives of those you've hurt.

Let God guide you in your need to use discretion in the forgiving process.
- Patience is a must.
  - You may be wondering, "Why won't my spouse have sex with me"? Well, duh!
  - Especially in the case of sexual wrongdoings, you have violated a most sacred safe haven that was intended for you and your spouse as a married couple.

Marriage is honourable in all, and the bed undefiled: but whoremongers and adulterers God will judge. (Hebrews 13:4)

- Depending on how understanding your spouse is, it could be a long, frustrating road to regain that lost trust. Remember, however, that prayer can work wonders.
- Might your spouse be having concerns about STDs?
- A suggestion to be tested could also result in a sincere desire to regain that lost trust.

Developing Intimacy

There needs to be a period of time specifically for the development of a newfound intimacy between you and your spouse. My counselor gave us several exercises designed for this purpose. Each exercise should be followed by no sex for at least two hours. This would also be a good way to develop intimacy for *any* married couple.

- The objective here is to develop *intimacy*—not to have sex.
- For men, sex obviously comes easy; intimacy does not come as naturally and needs some work.
- Make every effort to be sensual in performing these exercises, don't simply go through the motions as a homework assignment, but try to be creative.

Homework assignments

1. **Spend 20–30 minutes rubbing lotions on each other's hands.** Take time to make this a sensual, affectionate experience which would ultimately define intimacy.
2. **Spend 20–30 minutes washing each other's feet.** Make it as intimate as possible, maybe using candles, body wash, soft music, etc.
3. **For a devotional exercise read The Song of Solomon.** Alternate verses, and take plenty of time.

Again, these exercises should be followed with *no sex* for at least two hours. *Intimacy* is the goal.

There are several other exercises designed to develop or enhance intimacy, but remember ... no sex for two hours afterward. This exercise is for intimacy only, not sex. These exercises should *not* be done one right after the other but rather over a period of several days, and even possibly a couple of weeks.

One of the effects of the sexual abuse is anger. If everything doesn't go exactly as planned, don't let your anger get the best of you. There may be a deep-seated cause as to why this may be a challenge. Remember, this violation was not her fault, and trying to turn her on like a light switch may not be an easy thing to do. There is nothing wrong with having a discussion. Ask her what may or may not be pleasing to her. Communication is one of the most neglected aspects of marriage; good communication is vital to a healthy relationship.

Because of my confusion regarding what "normal" was, I requested a list of things that, to her, were taboo and also what things were most pleasurable for her. There is nothing wrong with sharing what is and isn't acceptable to each other. Remember, the goal of each partner should be to make his or her mate completely fulfilled. Have an honest and open discussion, and if something you'd like to do would make her uneasy ... well, is that really what you want? Not getting your way is not a reason to seek gratification elsewhere.

Throughout this book, I have mentioned some of the effects adult men experience as a result of being sexually abused as children, such as difficulty with intimacy and the inability to maintain relationships. I've also come to realize that I have difficulty completing projects. I have always considered myself an "ideas" man but have actually acted on very few of these entrepreneurial ventures.

I have realized that we all have a great deal to contribute to the benefit of others. We have not only the Gospel to share, but we also have had some rather unappetizing ingredients in our lives that are all working together for good, according to Romans 8:28.

Through the terrible decisions I made all my life, error after error, I allowed the devil to score over and over against my feeble defenses. But now that I have won victory over this, it's a brand new ball game, and God will get the glory and ultimate victory when my story is shared with others.

Chapter 7

It's Not My Fault, But ...

The Little Guy

It is true that being a victim of sexual abuse as a little boy was not my fault. This is a significant truth to acknowledge on the road to a healthy recovery as a victim of sexual child abuse. One of the assignments I was given was to write a letter to "the little guy," the little boy inside me who experienced the sexual abuse. In this letter, "the little guy" must be assured that none of what happened to him as a child was his fault.

When first given this assignment, I thought it was kind of silly. After all, "the little guy" is long gone. But I found, after completing this project, that "the little guy," with the help of God, was actually quite helpful in recalling things I needed to have brought out.

A little boy is vulnerable to the coercion and manipulation of an adult, or even an older adolescent, whether it was a relative or a total stranger. This "little guy" must know that he is loved and that nothing done in the past, present, or future can change that. Just think how horrible it would be if God's love was *not* unconditional, and every time we tripped and fell, we would have to experience God's wrath rather than His mercy.

We must display that same kind of love to others and that

should begin with our ability to love ourselves. Love does not mean *approval*. The Bible commands us to love one another, but we don't have to approve of wrongful actions.

The following is a copy of my letter to "the little guy":

> Dear Blythe,
>
> I know that you have been experiencing things that make you feel dirty, guilty, and ashamed, and you don't understand why. I know that these things feel good to your body, but you are confused because it also makes you feel dirty, guilty, and ashamed. I want you to know that *all* of these things happening to you are in *no way* your fault. You have been manipulated to do things that make you feel this way.
>
> You have been a victim of sexual abuse by someone you trusted and looked up to. Your uncle has caused you to do things that should only be done by married grown-ups. *This is not your fault* because you didn't know any better. Even though these things feel good, you know deep down that they are wrong, and that has made you confused. Being confused is not wrong, and you did nothing wrong, because a trusted older uncle manipulated you into doing this. Just because this has happened does *not* mean you are a bad boy or that you are unlovable. I *love you* very much!
>
> Blythe, you must understand that *none* of these things and nothing else you could tell me would keep me from loving you. I love you as much as if this had never happened. I need for you to help me now because I am trying to understand

how this thing that has happened to you has now affected me.

Even though I'm not sure that I *want* to remember some of the things that happened, I really do *need* to know if there is something I don't remember. Can you tell me if anyone else has been with you and Uncle [name omitted], or if anyone saw you doing "your secret" and didn't say or do anything?

I'm having a terrible conflict trying to deal with those things that have happened to you and how they are hurting me even now. I am praying that God will use you to help me recall *anything* that will help me to get victory through this. You have been given the chance to play a very big role in helping with this, and when it is all behind us, we will both give God the glory for it all. I cannot begin to express how much I love you and would like to have been there to help you with your struggle. You can now be there to help me in a way that I couldn't be there for you. I wish I could take you in my arms and hug you. I want to assure you that you are loved more than you can know, and *nothing* in the past, present, or future could keep me from loving you.

I love you,
Blythe (The Big Guy)

It is incredible how God has used "the little guy" in my life to bring to the forefront of my mind many suppressed memories. These recollections have subsequently given me the strength to address several issues, bringing continual healing to me.

I remember one day when I was sleeping, Sabrina came in

when she heard me tossing and turning and obviously having some kind of dream. Sabrina is a second-degree black belt in Tae Kwon Do, and we had started a class at our church as an outreach ministry. I learned a little but am not near as proficient as Sabrina. When she woke me up I was right in the middle of the dream so it was easy for me to remember: I had just seen my uncle abusing "Little Blythe," and I (grown-up Blythe) gave my uncle a Tae Kwon Do kick to protect "the little guy." This was quite a victory for me, both because I was able to help "the little guy" and also because I didn't fall on my face doing the kick.

A Child No More

Eventually, there comes a time when our baggage, no matter how horrific, needs to be dealt with, and one must be held accountable for one's own actions. This truth should be applied in other types of addiction also. Whether it is an addiction with alcohol, drugs, pornography, or any other vice that controls one's action, we must come to grips with the fact that we are now adults and need to take ownership of the things we do or have done.

As children, we go through a learning process. For example, we learn to do various chores, like picking up our toys and putting our clothes away. When a two-year-old does not display this discipline, we understand that this is just a child. When this same child grows into a teenager, that lack of discipline becomes a lot less acceptable. The Bible teaches that we must all eventually put away those childish things.

> When I was a child, I spake as a child, I understood as a child, I thought as a child: but when I became a man, I put away childish things. (1 Corinthians 13:11)

While it is true that abusive experiences tend to cause much more deep-seated issues than that of simply not picking up your toys or clothes, this same principle applies to victims, whether of sexual, physical, or verbal abuse, or whatever baggage one might be carrying. We must put away those childish things.

The Bible teaches that we are *all* sinners (Romans 3:10) and that there is a penalty to be paid for our sins (Romans 6:23a).

Distasteful Ingredients

My former pastor once used the following example to explain how all things are working together for good: In order to bake a cake, you need many ingredients, such as eggs, shortening, flour, baking powder, salt, and sugar. If you were to take just a spoonful of shortening, baking powder, salt, or even a raw egg by itself, it would not be very tasty. However, when you add *all* the ingredients together and follow the instructions, the end product will be a nice, fluffy, delicious cake.

In order to have a God honoring and glorifying life (comparable to the fluffy delicious cake), we all experience different ingredients day by day, such as sexual abuse, depression, success, physical abuse, failure, and victory. We then wait for *God's* timing for the end product.

If you focus on (or "taste") the abuse, depression, defeats, or failures, it will not be very appetizing; however, when you consider that God uses *all* the ingredients and allow for *His* direction and timing, then He will develop an end product that will be pleasing, honoring, and glorifying to Him.

Remember, whether for a cake, or for life:

> And we know that *all things* work together for good to them that love God, to them who are the called according to His purpose. (Romans 8:28, emphasis added)

God's Program

As human beings, we tend to categorize sins by their degree of wickedness. While it is true that some sins result in more severe consequences, we still need to understand that *all* sin is punishable by eternal separation from God. The only true peace is the peace that can only be provided by forgiveness through the shed blood of Jesus Christ. God sent His son to pay the penalty for our sin.

> For God so loved the world, that he gave his only begotten Son, that whosoever believeth in him should not perish, but have everlasting life. (John 3:16)

Salvation is *totally free!*

There are some programs out there that will take you through a logical, step-by-step process to overcome whatever sin it is that may have its grasp on you. Although these groups can be very beneficial in helping you overcome addictions, no program can provide the true peace that only God can provide through the sacrifice of Jesus Christ.

My father used to tell me that nothing in life is free, and that is for the most part true. But there are two glorious facts about God's program. First of all, it is truly free. The peace that passes all understanding is totally *free!* It says so in the Bible (emphasis added).

- "For God so loved the world, that He *gave* His only begotten Son, that whosoever believeth in Him shall not perish, but have everlasting life" (John 3:16).
- "…but the *gift* of God is eternal life through Jesus Christ our Lord" (Romans 6:23).

- "For by grace are ye saved through faith; and that not of yourselves: it is the *gift of God*: *not of works* lest any man should boast" (Ephesians 2:8–9).

Eternal "Lifetime Guarantee"

A lot of infomercials claim to offer a "lifetime guarantee." The second truth about God's program is that it has a lifetime guarantee and more. The difference is the guarantor, the one making the guarantee (or promise). These infomercial products are made by human hands and from things of this earth. Here's what the Bible says (emphasis added):

> Heaven and earth shall pass away: but *My* words shall not pass away. (Luke 21:33)

"My words" would include the promise that we can have everlasting life.

> For God so loved the world, that He gave His only begotten Son, that whosoever believeth in Him shall not perish, but have *everlasting* life. (John 3:16)

> And I give unto them *eternal* life; and they shall never perish, neither shall any man pluck them out of my hand. My Father, which gave them me, is greater than all; and *no man* is able to pluck them out of my Father's hand." (John 10:28–29)

Yes, God's gift of salvation is completely *free*!

By applying the truths of God's program, you can break the bondage of whatever horrific experiences you were subjected to.

You can use whatever "ingredient" that God has deemed necessary in your life to produce a new God-glorifying legacy that you can then pass on to your children. The beginning of breaking this horrific experience is to make the conscious decision to:

Realize that you are a sinner: As it is written, There is none righteous, no, not one (Romans 3:10).

Realize that there is a price to be paid for your sin: For the wages of sin is death; **(R**omans 6:23a).

Realize that God loves you so much that He paid that payment through the shed blood of Jesus Christ on the cross: But God commendeth His love toward us, in that, while we were yet sinners, Christ died for us. **(**Romans 5:8).

Repent from your sin. *Repent* means to turn away from something and turn to something else. God wants you to turn *from* the things that have controlled you and turn *to* Him so that He can take control of your life.

> Then Peter said unto them, Repent, and be baptized every one of you in the name of Jesus Christ for the remission of sins, and ye shall receive the gift of the Holy Ghost. (Acts 2:38)
>
> I tell you, Nay: but, except ye repent, ye shall all likewise perish. (Luke 13:3)

Respond to God's invitation to receive this free gift.

> That if thou shalt confess with thy mouth the Lord Jesus, and shalt believe in thine heart that God hath raised him from the dead, and thou shalt

be saved. For with the heart man believeth unto righteousness; and with the mouth confession is made unto salvation. For whosoever shall call upon the name of the Lord shall be saved. (Romans 10:9–10, 13)

Upon making this decision, you now have a new life in Christ Jesus.

> Therefore if any man be in Christ, he is a new creature: old things are passed away; behold all things are become new. (2 Corinthians 5:17)

This does not mean you will not experience some of the same temptations you have had in the past, but it does mean that you have the Holy Spirit dwelling in you to help you overcome these temptations.

> Know ye not that ye are the temple of God, and that the Spirit of God dwelleth in you? (1 Corinthians 3:16)

With the help of God and His Holy Spirit, and through the salvation provided by His Son, Jesus Christ, you can be victorious over any of these sins that have been continually dragging you down. There are also good Christian counselors who have gone through the very things you are experiencing. They can be instrumental in providing some direction to face your challenges.

There are some things that you should and shouldn't do to help your ability to overcome this sin that doth so easily beset you. If someone has been plagued with alcoholism, however innocent it might seem, it would not be a good idea for him to "meet the guys" down at the bar. This would be throwing himself right back into an environment that would lend itself to a fall back into that addiction. The same would be true of one who has problems with pornography; going back to adult bookstores would only promote a fall back into that sin.

So, you might ask, what *can* I do? The Bible tells us:

> Watch ye and pray, lest ye enter into temptation. The spirit truly is ready, but the flesh is weak. (Mark 14:38)

Be constantly aware of your surroundings and the potential to fall back into sin. Watch out for those whom you know would encourage you to fall, and stay away from "secret places." If Adam and Eve had a second chance to not partake of the forbidden fruit, don't you think they would probably watch out for serpents and stay completely away from the tree of the knowledge of good and evil?

> There hath no temptation taken you but such as is common to man: but God is faithful, who will not suffer you to be tempted above that ye are able; but will with the temptation also make a way to escape, that ye may be able to bear it. (1 Corinthians 10:13)

Don't allow yourself to be caught in a situation that could cause you to return to that sin. God has moved into your life in the person of the Holy Spirit, and He will remind you of the things you should and shouldn't be doing. Be sensitive to the Holy Spirit. Daily devotions are a vital part of a life that will be able to resist these temptations.

> Memorize scriptures like these that will help you realize that God is with you always (this list is in *no way* comprehensive):

> Know ye not that ye are the temple of God, and that the Spirit of God dwelleth in you? (1 Corinthians 3:16)
>
> That Christ may dwell in your hearts by faith; that ye, being rooted and grounded in love. (Ephesians 3:17)
>
> To whom God would make known what is the riches of the glory of this mystery among the Gentiles; which is Christ in you, the hope of glory. (Colossians 1:27)
>
> Jesus answered and said unto him, If a man love me, he will keep my words; and my Father will love him, and we will come unto him, and make our abode with him. (John 14:23)
>
> But Christ as a son over his own house: whose house are we, if we hold fast the confidence and the rejoicing of the hope firm unto the end. (Hebrews 3:6)

After all is said and done, if you have genuinely repented and accepted the free gift of salvation, God lives inside you in the person of the Holy Spirit. As He lives inside you, He will make you extremely uncomfortable when you ponder doing things you shouldn't. Uncomfortable is not a bad thing here, as it will keep you from wanting to do things you know you shouldn't, help you avoid more adverse consequences.

I remember, as a young boy, falling on the playground and expressing to my teacher how it would be nice if we never had pain after scraping our knee or something like that. A wise teacher indeed, she explained to me that pain is a good thing in that it tells your body when medical attention is needed. If you cut or scrape yourself and it doesn't hurt, it could go unattended and become infected, which could lead to more negative consequences.

The same is true with being uncomfortable when the Holy Spirit confronts you regarding things you shouldn't be doing. If we pay attention to that uncomfortable feeling, we can avoid further negative consequences. This uncomfortable feeling is the Holy Spirit giving us a first warning of what may be in store if the sin continues unchecked.

Remember, we still have to live in these mortal bodies, and we will continue to sin. Just like we need to take a physical bath or shower every day to get the dirt off, we also need to have a spiritual cleansing. In the book of 1 John, there is a passage that I once heard called "The Christian's Bar of Soap."

> If we confess our sins, He is faithful and just to forgive us our sins, and to cleanse us from all unrighteousness. (1 John 1:9)

Chapter 8

Post-Game Review

I have learned many things about others and myself through this experience. I've learned that God was indeed correct when He had the apostle Paul penned these words:

> And we know that all things work together for good to them that love God, to them who are the called according to His purpose. (Romans 8:28)

I have read, and even shared with "head knowledge," this verse for many years. But when I was hit with this turn of events, I must be honest, I had a hard time, in my heart, imagining what good could possibly come from it.

God has brought me to the point of realizing my need to genuinely repent, and I received Christ as my Savior. God has brought me closer to Him than I had ever been before. God has given me direction, as far as what path I need to take, to determine what His ultimate plan is for my life.

My sincere desire is that the examples shared in this publication may be helpful to those who have gone through similar experiences. For me to go through this ghastly ordeal and not warn others when signs are detected would be comparable to not warning someone to get off the tracks when a train is coming.

A Special Point to Parents/Grandparents of Young Children

If you have not been victimized, but you have young children, please *protect those children* by any means necessary. The times we live in are scary, especially if you are trying to raise children. I see the influence that television has in the thoughts of these little minds and can't help but consider this: no one in their right mind would give a six-year-old the keys to their car, and no one in their right mind would expose a six-year-old to a sexual environment that is reserved for married couples. In each case, it *will* result in disaster.

Parents, *please* don't let your young children have access to things they have no business having contact with, whether it's inappropriate shows on television or suggestive dance moves in school. Yes, I have seen the results of little children being shown evocative and unsuitable gyrations in the public elementary school systems. It may all look cute, but consider that these things are much like the words that kids have been known to repeat that are not in the best interest of the children. Have you ever heard someone ask—or perhaps you've even asked your own children—"Where did you hear that?" Ironically, they learn most of their vocabulary from Mommy and Daddy.

I remember when I was in about the third grade, and my teacher had written two similar sentences on the chalkboard. She wanted someone to tell her which one was correct, and as a young, eager student, I raised my hand. "I know, I know!" The teacher called on me and I correctly identified the appropriate sentence.

She then asked, "Why is that the correct sentence?" She wanted me to explain all the verbs, nouns, and other parts of speech.

I didn't have a clue about that, but I knew that it was right, so I told her, "Because it *sounds* right." This was not the answer she was looking for, but to the credit of my mother and father, because they spoke proper English around the house, I knew how it should sound.

This example works the same way with those little ears hearing things they shouldn't be hearing, and little eyes seeing things, and then *doing* things, they shouldn't be seeing or doing.

We live in an age where we must be aware of our surroundings all the time. I was never more aware of this as when I heard of the problem of child trafficking. I have recently heard two incidents. In one, a man and his daughter were being "cased out" at hardware store. In another, a mother noticed a nine-year-old girl trying to give candy to her four-year-old daughter. This was being orchestrated by a man from quite a distance away. He was signaling the nine-year-old to continue pursuing the little girl.

It's times like these when we need to pray for God to protect our children and grandchildren, but we also need to be vigilant in doing our due diligence.

From a Crack to a Grand Canyon

Sabrina and I were driving one day when I saw a crack in the street and I noticed that it had gotten bigger. The crack had gone unattended, and water had seeped in, causing it to become bigger and bigger. I try to draw an analogy whenever I can, so I shared with Sabrina, "There's a good application there." If the crack in the road is not repaired, water will get in and the crack will expand and turn into a bigger crack, or even a pothole.

Just like with the crack in the road, if we give Satan even the smallest opening to seep in, he will use whatever means he can as a foothold into our lives for his destruction. Because the "crack" in my life had not been addressed and dealt with, it grew bigger and bigger until my "Grand Canyon" began to fall in on me.

Please don't give Satan a foothold into the lives of your children or grandchildren. Some things seem so innocent but are like the first little crack before the erosion begins. Children grow up faster than you can imagine, and they will be exposed to all that worldly influence too soon anyway. This world is difficult enough to survive in without having to deal with inappropriate images that will forever be ingrained in those little minds. Don't give the six-year-old child the keys to your car.

I do believe in the sovereignty of God, and that His will is being accomplished all the time; however, in my mortal, finite mind, I can't help but wish none of this had ever happened to me, and that I might have had a "normal" life. This example keeps ringing in my mind: introducing a six-year-old to a sexual environment that is reserved for married couples is like giving a six-year-old the keys to your car; in each case, disaster is imminent.

I am certainly glad that I was not given the keys to the car as a six-year-old, but my exposure to a sexual environment intended for adult married couples and the subsequent devastation has been disastrous.

I'm not looking for a shoulder to cry on or sympathy of any kind. But I can't help but consider the greater consequences all this has created. I have caused pain and countless adverse effects to many in my life as a result of my sexual abuse.

As so eloquently written by John Newton, "Amazing Grace— how sweet the sound that saved a wretch like me." The word *wretch* has come to be more applicable than ever since I began to document my story. It is only by the grace of God that my wretched past could ever be used as an ingredient to help create an acceptable, abundant, and healthy God-glorifying life.

Looking back to that little boy living in the *Ozzie and Harriet, Father Knows Best*, or *Leave It to Beaver* ultra-functional home, it had never occurred to me that something could be wrong with me, mentally speaking. Even so, I kept wondering all my adult life, *Why can't I kick this thing?* Why did I continually hear the same broken record that Paul wrote in Romans 7, paraphrased, "The things I would not do, those are the things I do, and the things I know I should do, those are the things I don't do." This makes me realize how much I must rely on God on a *daily* basis.

Before "our little secret" was revealed through my wife's love, endurance, and determination, I never even considered that I might have a problem. *Don't all men have issues with inappropriate sex?* I thought. *After all, that's the way God made us, isn't it?*

I've heard many times that one key to being successful over an addiction is simply to admit that you have a problem. I had suppressed a lot of contemptible things that had happened in my early childhood that had subsequently affected much of my adult life. I remember the first time I heard myself say it out loud: "I have a sexual addiction." It was another unappetizing ingredient that only God could use to shape me into what *He* wants me to be. Some people think the idea of having a sexual addiction is funny or just nonsense. Hollywood has tried to romanticize it, making its victims into charismatic rakes and playboys. I know this addiction is real, and the effects it causes to so many people are in no way funny.

A good pastor friend of mine said he could help my situation but only as he had study it, in theory. I shared with him that he would not want to actually experience this. No matter what some might believe, the consequences of this addiction are devastating.

No matter what you may have done and how much you think you are unforgivable, unlovable, or beyond the realm of redemption, God can still work it *all* for good.

I earnestly believe that God does, in fact, use *all things* for good, and I'm now going through a process to determine exactly how He will use this "ingredient" in my life. One of the things I've become extremely sensitive to is the necessity for parents to protect their children.

When all this was happening to me, it was usually in a great big house where there were several children and "stayovers" commonly occurred. Because of the many cousins, there were usually not enough beds to accommodate all of us, so we were often doubled up with someone at night.

I would conveniently be paired up with my uncle. There was one incident when another older uncle popped his head in to check on us around bedtime. He must have noticed something, because he said something like "you boys be good now." The implication was that we were doing "our little secret."

Children *must* be given complete liberty to share if there are *any* inappropriate secrets. I was afraid that my parents would punish me because I knew what I was doing was wrong, even though I was coerced into doing so by a trusted uncle. I don't believe I can overemphasize the importance of encouraging our children or grandchildren to be cautious when hearing phrases like "our little secret." The results of harboring, suppressing, or in any way hiding this kind of secret can, and probably will, be detrimental to one in later years. Remember: introducing a six-year-old to a sexual environment that is reserved for married couples is like giving a six-year-old the keys to your car; in each case, disaster is imminent.

This lifestyle was introduced to me at the age of six or seven and continued with my uncle for approximately six years. Because of the age and the length of time this occurred, the adverse outcomes compounded.

Some information can be helpful in identifying the struggles of adult men who are victims of sexual child abuse. These things have helped me in a couple of ways. I learned some of the root causes that contributed to my behavior. Before, I'd had no idea of these root causes, and I had difficulty understanding what "normal" sexual behavior was.

After doing extensive research on the subject of sexual abuse of boys and the effects on them as adult men, I created a list of some affects that I have personally experienced and some that have been shared by others, although it's certainly not all-inclusive.

Not every victim has the same outcomes, but these are

common consequences of adult men who have a history of being sexually abused. There is no way to foretell how people will be affected by abuse. Not everyone reacts the same way. However, we do know that sexual violence can have intense effects on men who were sexually abused as children:

- Feeling of low self-esteem.
- Difficulty making decisions.
- Inability to maintain relationships.
- Difficulty completing projects.
- Difficulty trusting others.
- Habitual dishonesty.
- Need to "prove" ability to perform.
- Insatiable sexual appetite.
- Feeling of "can't get enough."
- Feeling of "I've got to try that."
- Feelings of guilt.
- Feelings of shame.
- Feelings of inadequacy/impotence.
- Believing body type is not satisfactory for partners.
- Disregard for the feelings of and long-term effects on others.
- Uncontrollable anger.
- Numbness.
- Sense of loss, grief.
- Nightmares and insomnia.
- Anxiety and fear.
- Depression.
- Mood swings.
- Problems dealing with masculinity and gender identity.
- Use of alcohol or other drugs.
- Suicidal thoughts and behavior.
- Flashbacks and invasive thoughts.
- Other mental health issues.

The extent to which these troubles appear and the impact they have differs significantly among men who were abused as children.

I can confirm firsthand the following effects:

- Tendency to compare:
  - Partners—"*She* did this, why won't you do this?"
  - Physical attributes.
  - Inability to truly satisfy my wife—It becomes all about *me* and my needs.
- Inferiority regarding *my* physical attributes.
  - Resulting from exposure to other men who have caused me to question my own body.
  - The exposure planted seeds of doubt in my mind about my ability to truly be "enough." With a lot of reassurance from my wife, these doubts have now been minimized.
- Continual desire to try for a new high, sexually.
  - This is where the question regarding "what's normal" comes in. Because of a skewed view of "normal," I would find myself wondering, *Would this be offensive to her?*
  - I have requested a "taboo list" from my wife to help me determine what is and what is not acceptable. This will enable me to determine what "normal" would be for us.
- Issues with insecurity.
  - This will probably take a long time of healing as I find myself wondering, What must she *really* think of me?

Issues Associated with "Being a Man"

Some additional issues have been exaggerated by our culture regarding men who were sexually abused or assaulted.

Coping with sexual abuse sometimes means coping with a lot of misconceptions about "being a man" and other myths. (See chapter 11.) Some of the challenges and misconceptions men who were abused as children face are as follows:

- Pressure to "prove" manhood
    - Physically, by becoming stronger, bigger, and meaner (maybe a bully).
    - Engaging in dangerous, violent, or risky behavior.
- Confusion over gender and sexual identity
- Sense of being inadequate as a man
    - If the man is small in stature, it could accentuate his sense of inadequacy
- Feeling loss of power and control in relation to manhood
- Problems with closeness and intimacy
- Sexual problems in general
- Fear that the sexual abuse has caused or will cause him to become homosexual or gay
- Homophobia, fear or intolerance of homosexuality

During my research, I found a very helpful website that assured me that what I am experiencing is not uncommon for someone who was sexually abused as a child. The following is only a small part of the information on the website, but I feel this to be a very important fact to consider.

One of the concerns I have experienced is that others who are misinformed will believe the myth that those who have been abused will automatically (or at least by and large) become abusers. This belief is a complete fallacy.

From the website www.livingwell.org.au:

Addressing the Victim to Offender Cycle

Do boys who have been sexually abused go on to commit sexual offences?

In writing this page, we want to be clear up front that research evidence tells us that being sexually abused *does not* cause someone to sexually offend and that the majority of boys who are sexually abused *do not* go on to commit abuse.

However, this question, whether or not boys who have been sexually abused will go on to commit sexual offences, remains a serious concern that deserves careful consideration. Not just because it is important to consider all possible factors that contribute to sexual offending, but also because too often discussions of the *"victim to offender cycle"* do not adequately explore the impact of uninformed public discussion on the lives of men subjected to sexual abuse.

Unfortunately, this particular topic has been characterized by misinformation and overly simplistic treatment. There is a common belief that being sexually abused *causes* a boy to become sexually abusive. As a result, many men who have suffered sexual abuse are faced with often overwhelming fear of becoming a perpetrator.

It is a telling observation that of all the possible outcomes of the sexual abuse of boys (such as depression, anxiety, flashbacks, relationship difficulties, disturbed sleep, suicidality, post trauma distress, etc.) the risk of later sexual offending is one of the most researched.

I encourage you to visit this website for more information about this subject.

A Special Note: To all those who have been adversely affected as a result of my experience and subsequent behavior, I pray that you too will realize that *all* things work together for good and that, however unappetizing these experiences have been to you, God is working for good in His time. I am truly sorry for any grief and hurt I have caused, and I pray that the rewards will be plentiful for having been subjected to these un-pleasantries.

As much as I would love to wrap my arms around that little boy who was the victim of this abuse, I too would like to collectively wrap my arms around all those whom I have hurt. Remember, we do have a God whose arms can reach around all of us.

Chapter 9

Getting a Grip

Forgive and accept forgiveness
I. Get it settled with God

1. Admit that you have this problem to deal with.
   - Half of solving the problem is admitting you have one.
   - Regardless of whether or not the root cause is your fault, there are some issues you must confront and deal with.
2. God's intervention is possible.
   - There is a peace that passes all understanding that is only available through the love of God Himself.

So many people struggle with the question, "Can I really *know*, or do I have to just do the best I can and hope it was enough?" The Bible teaches that we can know that we can be forgiven and have eternal life.

> These things have I written unto you that believe on the name of the Son of God; that ye may know that ye have eternal life, and that ye may believe on the name of the Son of God. (1 John 5:13)

Consider the five steps as previously mentioned as "The Romans Road"

While it is incredibly liberating to have your sins completely forgiven and paid for, that does not mean there will not be temptations; however, we can overcome them.

> But every man is tempted, when he is drawn away of his own lust, and enticed. (James 1:14)

> There hath no temptation taken you but such as is common to man: but God is faithful, who will not suffer you to be tempted above that ye are able; but will with the temptation also make a way of escape, that ye may be able to bear it. (1 Corinthians 10:13)

II. After getting your eternal destiny settled, you still need to resolve the effects of being sexually abused.

The following are some exercises that were assigned to me by my counselor and were very helpful:

1. **Write a letter to your abuser; don't keep anything back at all.** Tell him or her how much you have been hurt and how he or she had no right to do this to you. Feel free to use any expletives necessary to get your point across.
   - After completely venting all the venom you have in you, take the letter and throw it in a fireplace; burn it.
2. **Write a letter of forgiveness to your abuser.** Explain in the letter that you have accepted God's forgiveness and that you want to be like God and therefore, forgive your abuser. "And forgive us our debts as we forgive our debtors" (Matthew 6:12).

- Remember, failure to forgive someone is only hurting you. The one who transgressed against you doesn't even know that it is affecting you.
- After writing this letter of forgiveness, burn it.

You may actually find it surprising to see that the letter of condemnation could be more difficult to write than that of forgiveness. I was pleasantly surprised to see that was the case for me. In either case, remember that forgiveness is a *must* for you to be completely free of your abuser.

III. Inside all adults is a little child who still has conflicts and holds an incredible amount of power when it comes to controlling and potentially healing you (the adult).

Here are some things that have helped me "tap into" the "little guy".

1. I can't overemphasize the benefits of writing. Get a pencil and paper and write your story. You may experience dreams that will reveal some of the things that have been trapped in your subconscious mind. Have a notepad and pencil near your bed so you can easily jot them down as soon as they come. If you wait, you will probably not remember later when you wake up.
   - You should attempt to see your story through the eyes of the "little you."
   - This may be somewhat difficult because you have a lot of "stuff" in your subconscious mind.
   - This story is for your benefit and for future reference; it will not need to be burned, so guard it carefully. Expression of intimate details may be very helpful, so make sure it is not left lying around.

- Your goal here is to recall all the details as they happened.
2. After writing down your story, write a letter to the "little you." There is a sample of the letter I wrote to "The Little Guy" in chapter 7.
    - You should focus on assuring this "little you" that he/she was in *no way* to blame for what happened.
    - Assure him/her that nothing that happened then, now, or in the future would prevent you (the adult) from loving the "little you."
    - Explain to the "little you" that you would like to have been able to help while all this was happening.
    - Ask the "little you" to help you (the adult) remember things that could help you now in the healing process.
    - Be prepared for a potential shock.
    - There are things in your subconscious that you may not *want* to know but that you *need* to know in order to continue healing. You may ask some of the following questions:
    - Was anyone else involved in the abuse, either another being abused or another participating abuser? It's possible there was a third party during your abuse.
    - Did someone know what was happening but did nothing to help?
3. Pray for God to direct the "little you" to help you recall anything. You might discover some things that are quite disturbing, for example:
    - You might find that someone you hold very dear was either a participant or had some knowledge of the abuse and neglected to help. You have simply blocked it out of your mind. For me, I can still see a shadow of a third person, but God has chosen not to have that third shadow revealed. It could be that I'll never know.

- It may be that you continued on with someone other than your initial abuser.
- Be prepared; you may reveal things that cause you to become aroused and subsequently feel a sense of guilt. After all, you were supposedly abused, so why would you feel good about it? Remember, this is a natural and normal sensation.
- Because of the disturbing nature of your discoveries, you may experience extreme emotional lows ... *and* highs.

Dealing with Anger

IV. Some ways to deal with some of the aftereffects of having been sexually abused:

1. Anger is a very common problem for victims of child abuse. This is not to suggest that if one has an anger problem, they were subsequently abused as a child. Advice that I was initially given to deal with the anger was to simply stop the act of "erupting."
   - I liken this to going down the highway at seventy miles per hour and then trying to throw it into reverse.
   - Rather than "throwing it in reverse," it was suggested that I just take the off-ramp, figuratively speaking.
   - This was actually quite helpful to me. In reality, one generally has a sense of when they may be progressing (or digressing) to an eventual "explosion."
     - When I would get a feeling of frustration that I could tell was leading to an "explosion," I would gather myself and analyze exactly what was causing the frustration.
     - This is similar to married couples getting upset about little things, like squeezing the toothpaste

tube in the middle. There is something bigger going on, and this is simply a symptom of that bigger issue.
- Dealing with the anger before it got to the point of explosion was extremely exhilarating and gave me a sense of victory over the anger. Victory over the anger feels *much* better than exploding.
- My counselor suggested another trick to controlling anger: giving it the time test. Will I even know what I was so upset about in ten minutes, tomorrow, or the next week? It's generally not that big of a deal. After getting the initial "stuff" cleaned out of our system, these things will not seem to be that important anymore.
- Another trick is kind of like the WWJD (what would Jesus do) practice.
    - If someone cuts me off in traffic, because the Holy Spirit lives within me, I realize that they didn't just cut *me* off, but they cut *God* off too ... and if He didn't strike them dead, what am I getting so excited about?
2. Low self-esteem stems from several of the other adverse effects, such as the inability to maintain relationships or trust others and feelings of guilt or shame.
    - One thing that has helped my self-esteem is writing down things as they come to my mind. This helps me focus on things; as "the little guy" reveals them to me, I can then deal with them in a positive manner.
    - Sharing with confidants is another good avenue, and you should be receiving encouragement and positive feedback as your progression improves. Make sure you can trust the person you are confiding in—you don't need the surprise of finding your story on social media.

- Even during the writing of this work and sharing my story with others, I have found several who know someone who experienced sexual abuse as a child.
- I am convinced that there are a lot more sex addicts than we realize; however, there is more of a sense of shame and guilt simply due to the nature of this addiction. The addiction is usually initiated by the introduction of a sexual environment at an early age.
- Both alcohol and drug abuse, while horrific in their own right, are considered to be more of a social sickness and are more self-inflicted. Because they are social in nature, they are typically not a big secret to others.
- On the other hand, sexually abused children are rendered totally vulnerable because children have little power over the ones abusing them. That is not to say the other forms of addiction are not real, but children have very little say in the matter when they are introduced to a sexual environment designed for adult, married couples.
- Whichever addiction that may have afflicted you, either directly or as a victim of the victim, there *is* the potential for full and complete recovery from any such addiction.

Refer again to *Easy Living, Living The Lord's Prayer* by Rick Blue and *Breaking The Bondage of Addictions* by Mike Keller.

Chapter 10

Restoring Relationships

One of the tragic consequences of child sexual abuse is the effect it has on others in your life. As I mentioned before, I have continually demonstrated a disregard for the feelings of and long-term effects on others. Some relationships can be restored with a little effort on the part of both parties, but some restoration will be much more difficult. In either case, extensive prayer would be a good starting point. Restoration with your spouse is your ultimate goal. If contacting someone from your past in an effort to restore a relationship with them in turn plants seeds of mistrust for your spouse, don't pursue it.

After settling your eternal destination with God, the next act of restoration should be focused on your spouse. Reestablishing trust is critical in this process, and this will most likely take time. Trust is not earned quickly, and you should naturally expect the rebuilding of broken trust to take even longer. One of the positive things we can count on is that we *can* trust God. While I may fail and fail again, Sabrina has made it a point to trust God to protect her from further hurt.

OUR LITTLE SECRET, REVEALED

Some of the things I have done to help in the rebuilding of trust are as follows:

- I gave Sabrina complete control of my phone, email, and any other social media resource. Any hint of secrecy will only stifle the process of rebuilding broken trust.
- Whenever I feel a need to delete either a phone message or a text message, I make her aware, and we typically delete it together.
  I have learned this through our own rebuilding process. Even if it appears to you that it is nothing, she doesn't know that, and the breach of trust has caused the need for me to be above board with everything.
- Do *not* play the game of keeping score. "Well, I remember when you ..."

You must realize that this violation was not her fault, and anything brought up from the past will only add to the animosity that has already resulted from your behavior.

These may all seem a little drastic, but what I have done through my secret lifestyle has turned her world completely upside down. She thought she was married to a godly, churchgoing, upstanding, and trustworthy man. I sent her into a mental and emotional whirlpool. I must realize that I am constantly a work in progress in the hands of an Almighty God.

I remember, as a teenager, going to a seminar about conflicts that young people are typically faced with. One thing that stands out from that seminar is that we are all diamonds in the rough and that God is doing a work in all of us. All in attendance were given a button to remind us, and I have never forgotten the message of the button, which only has these letters: P.B.P.G.I.N.F.W.M.Y. If you've ever been to that seminar, you may remember what this means, but if not, it means this: please be patient; God is not finished with me yet. Until we reach our heavenly home, we are all a work in progress.

What about Sabrina?

One of the most devastating things about the effects of being sexually abused as a child is how it also affects the spouse. I consider myself extremely fortunate that Sabrina has been unbelievably understanding and supportive as an essential part of my healing process.

There are a few things I would like to point out that apply to rebuilding a healthy relationship once the dirty laundry has been aired. First of all, both partners need agree to draw a line in the sand, so to speak.

True forgiveness means being willing to forget things that occurred in the past. We do not have the same attributes as God, who can literally forget, but we should be willing to put any transgressions aside. By this, I mean there is absolutely no benefit for either of you to keep bringing up things from the past. Such actions would only hinder your lines of communication and, ultimately, the healing process. You should feel completely at liberty to discuss anything, and when something is mentioned that causes the other to respond, "Well, I remember when …," such things will only add debris that will clog up the communication pipeline. That has no benefit at all during this healing process. Remember, the healing process involves both of you. Drudging up the past is also comparable to ripping scabs off of old wounds, which would only cause further pain.

In the case of my wife and me, she had discovered things on my cell phone that made her suspicious about my inappropriate activity. Once it became a matter of record, and I had owned up to my activities, we agreed that after that date, we would no longer bring up the old stuff.

This also applies to blaming your spouse. "If you had … then

I wouldn't have." Focus on healing, not rehashing the cause of the problem.

One thing I did to ensure all the unwanted emails and text messages would stop was to close my email account. Nothing should prevent you from doing whatever it takes to restore your relationship. Remember, this was not the fault of your spouse.

Sabrina has been very helpful in holding me accountable. I have asked her to tell me if there is anything at all that causes her to be uneasy. This should be encouraged and should not result in a feeling of being "spied on" or as violations of privacy. Remember, this is not her fault.

As an example, after nailing down my relationship with God in salvation, I wanted to share with everyone, and as I discovered, many others had been struggling with their "assurance" of salvation. I had seen someone that I knew from my teen years on a social media site and began sharing my experience with her. I only shared my experience to the extent of "nailing down" my salvation, and I told Sabrina about it. She had no idea who this was and became curious, which made her uneasy. Because of her feelings, and because she is the most important person to me, I deleted all records of my sharing with this lady.

Although I thought this was the best thing to do, Sabrina later shared with me that one of the things that causes the distrust is the fact that I did delete all records. We have since made an agreement, first, for me to try to use better discretion when it comes to sharing with others (especially women). Second, if I feel the need to delete anything, I will let her see what I'm deleting first. This will reassure her that I am not attempting to keep any secrets. It also lends to promoting a rebuilding of the trust that has been violated due to my inappropriate actions. Again, I must remember that, as trivial as some of these things may seem to me, I am the one who caused this mistrust in the first place, and my main goal is to restore Sabrina's trust.

I have asked God to bring back to the forefront of my mind

anything that will help in my healing process. I have made a point to tell Sabrina everything as it is brought back to my recollection. Because of the nature of my past lifestyle, I must assure Sabrina that I am not trying to hide anything. When God brings things to the forefront, it may be manifested while you are asleep and cause some "interesting" dreams. I have been known to talk in my sleep, which will cause even more curiosity. Don't be afraid to express these things to your spouse. Focus on total honesty.

The more you work through getting all things in the open, the more you will notice these "inappropriate" dreams. I used an object lesson to teach kids how to clear the mind of the obscenity it may be filled with. I took a jar of tea (representing the dirty mind) and continued filling it with clean water (representing the word of God) until the jar became nothing but clean water. Scripture memorization is a vital part of the restoration of a clean mind.

If you are experiencing conflict due to child sexual abuse, pray that your spouse will consider that the original effects are not your fault. You still must realize the need to take ownership of your actions as an adult. While taking that ownership, you will have to deal with some inappropriate things, and some questionable events may result. Again, *pray* that God will intervene on your behalf. He does not want your marriage to fail; He would rather get the glory for a full restoration.

In a previous chapter, I mentioned writing a letter to "the little guy" and asking him to reveal things to me that I may not *want* to know but *need* to know. This will help me take appropriate actions in the healing process. Whenever "the little guy" brings something to my mind (usually when I'm sleeping), I will immediately share that with Sabrina.

Be sensitive to what your spouse is going through. While it is devastating for the one who has revealed a sexually abusive past and shared the horrific consequences, it is also devastating for the spouse who has stood by your side to that point. It may seem to her that I am now getting all the attention with therapy, extra love, and support. This may bring with it a feeling of "it's all about him," and the spouse now feels neglected. There must be a proper balance to ensure there are no feelings of bitterness because of all the attention you are now getting. It is possible that your revelation may actually trigger issues that your spouse had been dealing with but never shared. If that is the case you now both have the need for complete healing.

Referring back to the exercises for renewing the intimacy, be sure you don't try to rush the process of rebuilding the trust that has been taken from your spouse. A key point is to not blame your spouse for *your* inappropriate behavior; for example, "If you would ... then I wouldn't have to ..." Remember, it's not her fault.

Wounds that are caused by adulterous activity are very difficult to heal; it will take a long time to earn back the confidence that was lost. It will take both of you to rekindle a relationship. Try to remember how we are supposed to love our wives.

> Husbands, love your wives, even as Christ also loved the church, and gave himself for it. (Ephesians 5:25)

I try to do everything within my power to make sure Sabrina is the happiest person in the world. If I can make her the happiest person in our house, that's a start, and then she most naturally makes every attempt to please me too. That should not be your motive but rather a natural byproduct.

Many believe that marriage is a 50/50 proposition. This is completely erroneous, and believing it will only lend itself to an environment of "keeping score." Each partner should give 100 percent, with nothing expected in return. Think about Jesus Christ going to the cross. He gave 100 percent while knowing full well that He would be rejected, even by "His own."

He came unto his own, and his own received him not. (John 1:11)

She Needs Healing Too

We have sought different avenues from the wife's point of view to help Sabrina in the healing process. She has begun reading a Christian book on this very subject that has, to this point, proven very beneficial for her. My desire is that eventually, after we have gone through this process, we can both provide insight to couples (not just the men) that have a comparable experience. My prayer is that God will allow us to use this rather unappetizing ingredient in our lives to help others, and that God will ultimately get all the glory.

I remember, while going through my first divorce, that my mom and dad were compassionate, supportive, and tried to be understanding. Unfortunately, unless one has gone through a divorce, it is impossible to understand the things going through the minds of the divorcees. I have a cousin who had been through the experience of divorce several times, and I was able to get a different level of understanding and comfort from him because he had been down that road.

When it comes to credentials, I make no claims to such things as a PhD, counselor, pastor or even as an author. However, I believe that there is a reason God allowed these things to happen, and I want to provide understanding, direction, and comfort to others who have been subjected to these rather distasteful ingredients of life.

I have read the book *Healing Your Marriage When Trust Is Broken* by Cindy Beall, and it provides several true-life examples directly from couples who have gone through the horrific experience of infidelity. Men and women alike have strayed from their wedding vows. These examples are geared to help both spouses heal but focus mostly on the one who was the victim of the adulterous act.

As I look to how this story will exemplify Romans 8:28 in my life, I must consider the reality that God will use this rather distasteful ingredient to work together for His good, possibly in the area of simply sharing with others going through similar experiences.

Questions and Answers for Sabrina

Question: As you try to recover from this experience, what are some of the things you are doing?
Answer: Seeking God's guidance through scripture, Bible classes, church services, and listening to the Holy Spirit.

Question: In which areas do you feel trapped?
Answer: The inability to speak in depth with someone about what I was going through. Unable to focus on what was happening due to having to work twelve-hour days, fill commitments at church, and fill commitments for the family.

Question: What can you do to become un-trapped?
Answer: Continue to seek God for guidance, strength from the Bible, church, and Sunday school. Avoid letting anger, hurt, and bitterness control my thoughts and emotions.

Question: How do you feel about the idea that God is the only one who would never disappoint you?
Answer: I believe it whole heartedly. Too many times we put our trust and happiness in others, in jobs, or in success, but that is the flesh—the world. God is the only one who will never disappoint.

Question: Do you feel that is true to you?

Answer: Absolutely. Even through the most frightening and most devastating events that have happened in my life, I know it is God working his plan for me. Now, just because I said that, don't think I did not struggle. Each event has made me humble, sometimes brought me to my knees—which is where I should have been in the first place. But God has always made a way out, an escape. Each trial brought me out stronger and more understanding, sweeter, loving, and more dependent on God. My mother once said, "Sometimes God does a harsh pruning similar to the grapevines, only for them to come back stronger and healthier to flourish."

Question: In going through such a humiliating situation, what particular characteristics have you noticed that have surfaced in you?

Answer: At first I felt stupid. I wondered how this could happen to me again. I questioned myself—why did I not trust my instincts (the Holy Spirit)? I cried a lot. Begging God to help me. Sobbing uncontrollably. I felt weak, vulnerable like a wounded animal in the wilderness, and I was easy prey for the predators. Then my heart grew hard and very cold. I wanted to flee, leave in order to protect myself from any more potential hurt.

Question: Were you surprised, and if so, in what way?

Answer: I was not surprised with my reactions. Especially the fleeing part. That is what I'd done in the past.

Question: Do you believe you can ever get back to a "normal" marriage?

Answer: Normal? What is normal? Common? We have never had a common marriage. After a month of being married, we learned I had breast cancer, so the first two-and-a-half years was battling breast cancer. I think that is uncommon.

Question: If there is a "new normal" you may be anticipating, what would that look like to you?
Answer: I don't want normal, common, or an ordinary marriage. I believe we can have an extraordinary, uncommon, God-blessed marriage.

Question: As a result of the hurt you have experienced, do you believe your husband in any way planned to do this?
Answer: No. I don't think it started out that way. However, temptation, fleshly desires, and a distorted imagination led him to contact and chat with people. Once the contacts were made, the impulse to continue seeking and contacting others grew stronger. The drive to go further was unstoppable, and "the plan" was made to meet, and they did.

Question: Is there someone you can turn to when you are bombarded with immense sadness and grief? Who is that and how are they able to help in your healing?
Answer: God is my source and strength. Humanly speaking, because I know of no one with similar experiences that I can turn to, my only source is God.

Question: When you look at this suffering, what insightful instruction have you learned about life, about yourself, and about others?
Answer: God's answers are not on our time. I believe He gives the answers to us when we are able to handle them and not before. I have learned it is okay to be angry, hurt, or sad, but don't use those emotions to sin. All of these emotions are part of the human condition, but you have to choose to turn from the temptations of evil and trust in God to heal the anger, hurt, and sadness. God's time will heal all wounds. These types of events not only affect the couple; they affect other family members, like moms, sisters, daughters, sons-in-law, grandchildren, coworkers, and members

of your church. This will compound the issues. Family members may be angry at him for hurting you, some will not trust him, and some will not have him welcomed in their home. While some have a forgiving heart and will support you as you journey through to see what God has planned next.

Question: Does rebuilding trust even appear to be possible to you?
Answer: Absolutely!

Question: Do you feel like your husband is willing to reestablish the lost trust?
Answer: Yes, he is begging for it.

Question: What is your feeling about that?
Answer: I believe he is genuinely seeking to regain the trust.

Question: What steps can you take as a couple to come together and work toward a joint trust?
Answer: Communication. If I have a question, he answers it. No matter how insignificant it may seem, he will answer with no hesitation. If I feel uncomfortable about a situation, I bring it up to discuss it with him, and we come to a solution.

Question: How do you feel about making this private matter public through this publication, or simply in discussing it with others?
Answer: I would only do it to help others in similar situations.

Question: How do you believe the church could play a more active and positive role in the healing process of those going through similar circumstances?
Answer: Weekly or monthly meetings for struggling families, or even one-on-one meetings. Stop, seek God, hard core, to the

point, no sugar-coating, get to the root of the recurring problem, identify, and keep working at it until there is a peace.

Question: When this infidelity was brought out in our life, we made the decision to remove ourselves from a teaching position in the Sunday school. Do you believe that was the right thing to do?
Answer: Yes, I believe we needed to step down for a season to heal and learn more of what God wants to do with the next chapter in our lives.

Question: Do you feel we would ever be able to go back to a similar position?
Answer: Absolutely!

Question: Keeping in mind that "all things work together for good," what is your desired outcome through this entire ordeal?
Answer: To keep focused on God and for us to become stronger as a couple and to help others through their healing process.

Question: In what way do you feel you may be able to help other women who are going through a similar situation?
Answer: To be an encouragement, to give them hope that with God all things are possible. Focus on scriptures assuring us that healing is possible.

Question: In dealing with the fact that your husband had turned to men for gratification, does that make it more difficult, less difficult, or no different than if it were a "normal" affair with only women?
Answer: No difference. The vows of our marriage were broken; it doesn't matter with whom.

Question: When "our little secret" became "our little secret—revealed," was it easier to understand the root cause of this addiction with sex?

Answer: Yes, it made total sense.

Chapter 11

Facts and Myths

In researching this subject, I found a few helpful websites that put me at ease concerning some things a lot of people are misinformed about. I have been assured that many of the things people think about this subject are totally myths. Below is a list of "Facts and Myths" regarding men who were sexually abused as children; this list should be extremely helpful as you question some things that are many times misunderstood.

The following chart of was provided by the Rape and Abuse Crisis Center, and the credit is given to them accordingly. 701-293-7273 Website: www.raccfm..com

Myths and Facts about Child Sexual Abuse

#1 Myth:

Child sexual abuse occurs only among strangers. If children stay away from strangers, they will not be sexually abused.

Fact:

Statistics show 93 percent of juvenile sexual assault victims know their attacker. Family members account for 34.2 percent of all perpetrators, and acquaintances account for 58.7 percent. Only 7 percent of perpetrators are strangers to their victim.[1]

#2 Myth:

Children provoke sexual abuse through displaying seductive behavior.

Fact:

Seductive behavior is not the cause. Responsibility for the act lies with the offender. Children are not psychologically prepared to cope with repeated sexual stimulation.[2] Sexual abuse, therefore, exploits children who are not developmentally capable of understanding or resisting the abuse.

#3 Myth:

The majority of child sexual abuse victims tell someone about the abuse.

Fact:

It is estimated that 73 percent of child victims do not tell anyone about the abuse for at least a year, and 45 percent of victims do not tell anyone for at least five years. Some never disclose.[3] Child sexual abuse has been reported up to 80,000 times a year, but the number of unreported instances is far greater because children are afraid to tell anyone what has happened.[2]

#4 Myth:

Men and women sexually abuse children equally.

Fact:

Studies have shown the majority of child sexual abusers are men.[5] Men sexually abuse both female and male children, and despite a common myth, homosexual men are not more likely to sexually abuse children than heterosexual men.[5]

#5 Myth:

If the children did not want the abuse, they could tell their perpetrator to stop.

Fact:

Because children are often taught the importance of obeying adults, they generally do not question the behavior of an adult. Children are often coerced with bribes, threats, or use a position of authority.

#6 Myth:

All sexual abuse victims are female.

Fact:

Studies indicate that female children are abused more often than male children.[5] It is estimated between 25 and 33 percent of women have been sexually abused during childhood. Estimates for men are 10 to 16 percent.[4] Therefore, male children are also victims of sexual abuse.

#7 Myth:

Family sexual abuse is an isolated, one-time incident.

Fact:

Child sexual abuse is usually a situation that develops gradually over a period of time and occurs repeatedly.[6]

#8 Myth:

In family sexual abuse, the "non-offending" parent always knows what has happened.

Fact:

While some "non-offending" parents know and even support an offender's actions, because of a lack of awareness, many suspect something is wrong but are unsure what to do.

#9 Myth:

Family sexual abuse only happens in low-income families.

Fact:

Family sexual abuse crosses all classes of society. There is no race, social, or economic class that is immune to family sexual abuse.

#10 Myth:

Nonviolent sexual behavior between a child and an adult is not damaging to the child.

Fact:

Nearly all victims will experience confusion, shame, guilt, anger, and suffer from possessing a poor self-image. Child sexual abuse can result in long-term relationship problems as well. The long-term emotional and psychological damage of sexual abuse can be devastating.[2]

Bibliography

Beall, Cindy. *Heling your Marriage When Trust Is Broken: Finding Forgiveness and Restoration.* Eugene, OR: Harvest House Publishers, 2011.

Blue, Rick. *Easy Living: Living the Lord's Prayer.* Maitland, FL: Xulon Press, 2002.

Holy Bible, King James Version.

Keller, Mike. *Breaking the Bondage of Addictions: Uncontrollable Anger, Drug/Alcohol, Irrational Thinking, Sexual Sins.* Cleveland, TN: Rock of Ages Prison Ministry, 2000.

Living Well. "Addressing the Victim to Offender Cycle," https://www.livingwell.org.au/managing-difficulties/addressing-the-victim-to-offender-cycle/.

Rape and Abuse Crisis Center. "Myths and Facts about Child Sexual Abuse," https://www.raccfm.com/files/child%20sexual%20abuse.pdf.

Our Daily Bread ………………………….. Our Daily Bread Ministries

References from "Myths and Facts about Child Sexual Abuse":

1. Rape, Abuse, and Incest National Network: http://www.rainn.org
2. American Academy of Child and Adolescent Psychiatry: http://www.aacap.org/cs/root/facts_for_families/child_sexual_abuse
3. Darkness to Light: http://www.darkness2light.org/KnowAbout/statistics_2.asp
4. Medline Plus: http://www.nlm.nih.gov/medlineplus/childsexualabuse.html
5. American Psychological Association: http://www.apa.org/pi/families/resources/child-sexual-abuse.aspx
6. World Health Organization: http://www.who.int/violence_injury_prevention/resources/publications/en/guidelines_chap7.pdf

About the Author

Blythe Hardy was a victim of childhood sexual abuse and reveals this secret fifty-five years later. Hardy sought help from pastors, psychologists, professional counselors, and authors. Many of these resources offered help only in theory. The best counsel given was from those with comparable experiences. He lives in Kansas.

Made in the USA
Monee, IL
01 November 2024